# BUILDING
# A VIRTUOUS
# SCHOOL

# BUILDING A VIRTUOUS SCHOOL

Guided Reflections on Catholic Character Formation

## TED LAXTON

NOVALIS

© 2013 Novalis Publishing Inc.

Cover: Blaine Herrmann
Layout: Audrey Wells
Cover image: iStockphoto

Published by Novalis

Publishing Office
10 Lower Spadina Avenue, Suite 400
Toronto, Ontario, Canada
M5V 2Z2

Head Office
4475 Frontenac Street
Montréal, Québec, Canada
H2H 2S2

www.novalis.ca

Library and Archives Canada Cataloguing in Publication

Laxton, Ted     Building a virtuous school : guided reflections on Catholic
character formation / Ted Laxton.

Issued also in electronic formats. ISBN 978-2-89646-488-3

    1. Catholic schools.  2. Catholic teachers.  3. Faith development. I. Title.
LC473.L38 2013              371.071'2              C2013-901661-9

Printed in Canada.

We acknowledge the financial support of the Government of Canada through the
Canada Book Fund for business development activities.

5 4 3 2 1       17  16  15  14  13

Dedicated to all whose vocation is in the field of Catholic education, especially those who collectively enabled me in my ministry as principal at Sacred Heart School.

# ACKNOWLEDGEMENTS

I would like to thank the staff and students at Bishop Macdonnell Catholic High School, Our Lady of Lourdes Catholic High School, Sacred Heart Catholic Elementary School, The Holy Family Centre and the Wellington Catholic District School Board for the privilege of working with people of passion.

I would like to thank Novalis for being a significant voice of evangelization in the modern world and especially for encouraging me in my journey.

I would like to recognize the invisible hand of Anne Louise Mahoney, whose redacting skills are evident in the flow of the text.

I would like to acknowledge the significant role of religious, priests and deacons in my formation as a Catholic teacher, especially Sister Linda Gleason, Sister Doreen Kirby, Sister Marie Taylor, Father John Lambertus, Monsignor John Newstead, Father Dennis Noon and Dr. Peter Gittens.

I want to express my heartfelt appreciation to Peter Ingram, for walking with me for the past 37 years on our journey to Emmaus.

I would like to thank my father and mother, Edison and Shirley Laxton, for being my primary faith educators.

Finally, I would like to thank my wife, Terri, and our daughters, Caitlin, Merin and Brynn, for being so supportive throughout the compilation of not only my life, but this work as well.

# CONTENTS

Introduction .................................................................. 11

**THE THEOLOGICAL VIRTUES** ................................... 15

**I. Faith** ...................................................................... 16

    1. The Christmas Miracle .......................................... 17

    2. The Splendorous Flower ....................................... 21

    3. First Holy Communion .......................................... 25

    4. The Canvas of the Soul ........................................ 28

**II. Hope** ...................................................................... 31

    5. "Free Willy" ......................................................... 32

    6. The Iridescent Spring Peacock .............................. 34

    7. "Hi" ..................................................................... 36

    8. Rites of Passage .................................................. 38

**III. Love** ...................................................................... 40

    9. Mystery, Miracle and Loss ................................... 41

    10. EA .................................................................... 43

    11. The Gentle Gatherer ........................................... 45

    12. "I Love You" ...................................................... 47

**THE CARDINAL VIRTUES** ....................................... 49

**I. Fortitude** ................................................................ 50

    13. This Moment of Luminosity ................................ 51

14. The Breath of Life ........................................................ 54

15. Inspiration .................................................................. 57

16. Pastor of the Pasture .................................................. 59

## II. Justice ........................................................................ 61

17. The Axis Mundi ........................................................ 62

18. The Perfect Class ........................................................ 64

19. The "Multicoloured Tunic" ......................................... 66

20. You Shall Shine Like the Stars in Heaven ..................... 68

## III. Prudence ..................................................................... 70

21. The Spirit Chime ....................................................... 71

22. "Why Don't You Ever Take Me?" ................................. 73

23. "You Have Hidden These Things" ............................... 75

24. The Prudent Teacher .................................................. 77

## IV. Temperance .................................................................. 79

25. The Humblers ............................................................ 80

26. The Gift .................................................................... 82

27. Hidden Blessing ........................................................ 84

28. The Wolf and the Lamb .............................................. 86

## COMMUNAL VIRTUES ..................................................... 89

## I. Gratitude ........................................................................ 90

29. Thanks "For Me!" ...................................................... 91

30. "Glad and Generous Hearts" ...................................... 94

31. The Lord's Table ........................................................ 96

32. The School Village ..................................................... 98

## II. Compassion ................................................................. 100

33. My Staff, They Comfort Me ....................................... 101

34. Coming Ashore ........................................................ 103

35. Tributaries of the Soul .............................................. 105

36. The "Chill Grill" ...................................................... 107

**III. Discipleship** ...........................................................109

    37. Sacred Impressions ..........................................110

    38. Hearing Is Believing ........................................112

    39. Liberated from the Tombs ..............................114

    40. The Disciple's Mandala ...................................116

**IV. Reverence** ...............................................................118

    41. Mending Damaged Wings ...............................119

    42. In the Beginning, Order Was Created .............121

    43. "The New Girl's on Fire!" ................................123

    44. Cleanliness Is a Sign of Reverence ..................125

**V. Solidarity** ...............................................................127

    45. A Prize-winning Race .....................................128

    46. The "Seraphim of Song" .................................130

    47. Delilah's Demise .............................................132

    48. "Come, You That Are Blessed" .......................134

**VI. Stewardship** ...........................................................136

    49. Simon the Good Steward ................................137

    50. "TJ," Steward of the Imagination ...................140

    51. Sacred Footprints ...........................................142

    52. The Pontificator .............................................144

**How to Use This Book** ..................................................147

# INTRODUCTION

I n recent years, I've come to envision the development of Catholic character through the metaphor of dance. This dance contains three main elements: the partners of mind and heart, as well as the music of the soul. Our own character is a product of synchronizing our knowing, valuing and loving. We who are privileged to be educators are ever in need of harmonizing the steps of our dance with the music in our soul. I invite all educators to follow the steps provided in this book.

The Canadian Jesuit philosopher and theologian Bernard Lonergan said that one of the purposes of art is to pull "the subject out of his [or her] ready-made world, and [present] him [or her] with space.... [B]eing pulled out of one's ready-made world is a moment of withdrawal, of pause. Such moments are moments in which one can start afresh, release a new movement to the realization of one's own idea of being human, to the appreciation of what it is to be a Christian, a new movement towards his [or her] ideal."[1] I hope to provide all who read this book with a space like the one used by the artist – contemplative space.

This book is intended as a work of art in the sense that through the eyes of a Catholic principal, instances of religious experience are sketched in language that seeks to connect them with both the dynamism of the human spirit and Catholic tradition. The reflec-

---

1   Bernard Lonergan, *Collected Works of Bernard Lonergan*: Topics in Education; The Cincinnati Lectures of 1959 on the Philosophy of Education, vol. 10 of The Robert Mollot Collection, edited by Fredrick E. Crowe and Robert M. Doran (1993. Reprint. Toronto: University of Toronto Press, 2005), 223, 224.

tions are intended to draw educators out of the ready-made world of their regular duties to moments of withdrawal. Staff can reflect on the potential that exists within themselves and their vocations to become more authentic and, as a group, to form a more fully human Catholic community. All of the stories recounted in this text are based on things that happened in schools, but details are blurred to protect identities. The use of metaphor, analogy and symbol is intended to achieve what Lonergan calls the presentation of the "splendor of the world as a cipher, a revelation, an unveiling, [of] the presence of one who is not seen, touched, grasped … yet is present."[2] The methodology of this book employs the "art of linguistic expression," by which I mean a synthesis of the artist's experience of value and the writer's narration of that experience. I leave it to each person and community to appropriate the meaning of their own experiences and to deliberate on the best way to reorient their life and that of their community in response to those experiences, insights and affirmations.

The vocation of any person working in a Catholic school is a response to God's grace and God's call to live in loving relationship. This book is an attempt to support the ongoing formation needs of staff working in a Catholic school. It can be used as a moment for formation at any staff gathering (such as staff meetings), during days dedicated to spiritual development (such as spiritual development days or retreats), for courses whose aim is to form experienced or future teachers (such as religious education courses or Faculty of Education pre-service courses), and for courses whose aim is to form experienced or future principals (such as Catholic Principals' Council courses or Catholic Principal's Qualification Programs). Finally, and most importantly, these reflections are intended for personal growth through affirming your own religious experiences of the extraordinary within the "ordinary" context of your life. When you do this, you have begun the processes of conversion and reorientation.

The vignettes found at the core of this text are like spiritual parables with threads of value that form the patterns in our lives. The very act of coming to recognize the pattern woven by the threads requires that each person attend to the meaning of his or her own life experi-

---

2   *Ibid.,* 222.

ences and how they shape his or her way of being in the world. The ultimate pattern to be discerned in the tapestry of life is that of Jesus Christ. Your personal tapestry is an image of your own response to the love of God, the way of Jesus and the indwelling Spirit.

The questions used in the reflections incorporate Bernard Lonergan's transcendental precepts of being attentive, intelligent, reasonable and responsible, which yields cumulative and progressive results. The reflections serve several purposes to that end within the context of the mission of a school that is constantly seeking to transform itself. On the first level, they provide you with an awareness of the data of religious experience, as lived out in the daily life of the Catholic school. On the second level, you come to understand the emerging spiritual tapestry of your own religious experiences. On the third level, you come to affirm the reality of each virtue as a spiritual force in your own life and that of your community. On the fourth level, you reorient yourself and your school community by making personal and communal commitments, which lead to further personal growth and the transformation of the culture of the school.

Virtues are generally regarded to be habits that perfect the human mind, heart and soul. They take the form of intentions and acts that realize the good. I see parallels between our pursuit of the good and the biblical story of the Magi (Matthew 2: 1-12), which serves as an archetype of the human journey to self-transcendence through the process of conversion. The star represents the transcendent good toward which we humans, by the very dynamism of our being, are driven to pursue.

The virtues can be symbolically imagined as a constellation of stars that illuminate the good of our own transformation. The virtues described in this book are divided into three categories:

- the theological virtues—faith, hope and love (charity)

- the cardinal virtues—fortitude, justice, prudence and temperance, and

- six communal virtues—gratitude, compassion, discipleship, reverence, solidarity and stewardship—which function in harmony with the theological and cardinal virtues to form the character of both the person and the community.

When this conversion is accompanied by concrete acts of goodness, we begin to transform our earthly kingdom into a heavenly one. Eventually, through the pursuit of goodness (the star that the Magi followed), we may even glimpse the birth of a new consciousness of Jesus (God incarnate) in the ever-deepening state of being-in-love in an unconditional fashion (religious conversion). When this occurs, we can never return to the former earthly order (Herod), but seek another route to building a more loving Kingdom on earth. I wrote this book of reflections to affirm, in the intentions and acts of all those who work in the various niches of Catholic education, that their pursuit of virtue has a meaning and value that transcends the ordinary mandate of education and strives for the extraordinary mandate of integral human formation.

## ENCULTURATING CATHOLIC CHARACTER

Enculturation, in the school context, refers to our individual and collective efforts to understand and put into practice gospel values and the principal tenets of our faith. Enculturating Catholic character is an ongoing process. It is achieved through the daily commitments of all members to witnessing Catholic values and virtues, which form not only our character, but that of the school community. Catholic communities should be places of dynamic formation, which means that the ethos of the community is constantly being reoriented through the conscious efforts of its members. If not, it risks disorientation through the forces of a culture whose primary values are becoming increasingly subverted by a philosophy of secularism. This set of reflections provides a basis for both personal and communal discernment, as a way to consciously respond to God's grace and the call to conversion.

For guidance on how to use this book, as well as a list of eleven steps to the enculturation of Catholic character and an outline of the methodology employed, please turn to How to Use This Book, found at the end of the book.

# THE THEOLOGICAL VIRTUES

*Read the definition (to yourself or as a group) of the theological virtues to provide an overall context for the particular virtue.*

The theological virtues of faith, hope and love open our minds, hearts and souls to the loving presence of God. The reflections that follow speak of human responses to God's grace and show how we affirm the theological virtues through our acts of faith, hope and love.

# I. FAITH

*Begin by writing your own definition of faith.*

*Then read the following description (to yourself or as a group) before exploring any of the reflections in this section on faith.*

I used to teach religion and science classes back to back. Sometimes I would have the same students in each class. One day, after a science class on genetic screening and the dignity of the person, a student came up to me and said that she was impressed with the faith dimension of the lesson. When I asked why, as she had heard a similar version of the lesson in religion class earlier in the semester, she replied, "You had to say that in religion class, but you didn't have to say it in science class, so you must really believe it!"

Faith is the spiritual dynamism that seeks and responds to the love of God. We begin to realize that the deepest longings of our hearts are ultimately met only in the source of absolute love, which is God. We come to this realization through revelation, through intellectual pursuit and through opening our minds and hearts to the abundance of God's grace. The following stories illustrate the good works that are born of the transformative power of God's grace in our lives, as realized through our daily interactions with colleagues and the students in our care.

*Now reconsider your definition of "faith": Is there anything you would change? If you are facilitating a group situation, allow time for participants to share their definitions in small groups. Ask the groups to come up with a definition of faith and then share it with the large group. Invite the groups to record their definitions for posting in a "Virtues" corner.*

# 1. THE CHRISTMAS MIRACLE

*Read the scripture quote below.*

> What good is it, my brothers and sisters, if you say you have faith, but do not have works? Can faith save you? If a brother or sister is naked and lacks daily food, and one of you says to them, "Go in peace; keep warm and eat your fill," and yet you do not supply their bodily needs, what is the good of that? So faith by itself, if it has no works, is dead. But someone will say, "You have faith and I have works." Show me your faith apart from your works, and I by my works will show you my faith. (James 2:14-18)

*Reconsider your most recent definition of faith. Is there anything you would change? Groups: Allow time for discussion and feedback to the large group. Individuals: Journal your response.*

*Read the story below.*

Once again, our own jolly young elf (our ever-loving special education resource teacher) had organized the school's Christmas food drive. Many families, as usual, gave generously out of their abundance.

One morning, I was standing on the sidewalk in front of the school, waiting for the children to get off the buses, and trying to engage those who were not half-asleep in a morning greeting. Suddenly, I heard a desperate call, "Mr. Laxton, can you help me?" There was a tiny child from one of our primary classes who was loaded down with a backpack, snow pants, mitts and a large shopping bag. She was perched precariously on the bottom step of the bus, not able to negotiate the final step with all her baggage. I thought, as I watched her balancing on the threshold of the world, that if the truth be known, this child had enough challenges to weigh herself down without taking on additional baggage. But I was wrong. Her spirit was borne upon the wings of faith, hope and charity, due in no small part to a mother who, although she had her material struggles, was obviously nourishing the soul of her own holy issue.

When I grabbed the large shopping bag, I discovered that it was full of canned food for the food drive. My heart paused as I thought of the girl's mother: surely her pantry shelf was as bare as Mother Hubbard's. I was humbled, thinking that here is a family that knows what it is to do "without" and yet they knew better than I what to do "within." Knowing the pain of poverty, they gave out of their poverty. I helped the little girl carry the bag to the office, my heart bursting with joy at the example I had been shown.

The next morning, as I greeted the children coming off the bus, I heard once again the refrain, "Mr. Laxton, can you help me?" I looked up and saw that it was our same little cherub in the exact same situation. I began to worry: had she told her mom that she was bringing all this food? How could I ask her? This scene played itself out day after day. I was bamboozled by the cornucopia of cans that were harvested from the pantry and hearts of this "holy family." I began to ask around: how could she possibly be bringing so much food? Amid the shrugged shoulders and blank stares, I found my answer in who else but our ever-loving and ever-knowing secretary. She, too, had wondered about the source of this plentitude of cans and had engaged the mother in an inquisitive conversation. It turned out that our little cherub, in response to the daily announcements beckoning all to give what they could, had decided to solicit her neighbours to see if they could contribute to this worthy cause. Of her own volition, she went door to door in a neighbourhood that knew well the pains of scarcity, collecting cans from the collective goodwill of these kind people's pantries. Here, incarnated in this tiny catechumen, was a synthesis of faith and good works that witnessed to the true meaning of Christmas.

*Reflect on the story:*

Does the story strike a chord with your experience? If so, try to identify not only the chord, but also the underlying value. If not, does it strike a note of discord? If so, why?

- *If you are in a group situation, allow time for group feedback on a voluntary basis.*

- *If you are doing this on your own, journal your thoughts for later reflection.*

## ENCULTURATING CATHOLIC CHARACTER

### Experience

*Write your response to the statement below. If in a group, share your response with the group. Each group will select one story to share with the large group.*

Recount a time when the generosity of a fellow human being revealed that person's faith.

### Understanding

*Talk to a friend or, if in a group, partner with someone who knows you, to answer the question. If in a group, on a voluntary basis, share your response with the group. Have each group, on a voluntary basis, share one response with the large group.*

Have a colleague or a friend tell you which of your good works bears witness to your faith.

### Reflection

*Write your response to the personal (P) question below. If in a group, on a voluntary basis, share your response with the group. Groups may, on a voluntary basis, share a story with the large group. The facilitator may skip the personal question and move to the community (C) question. Each group should be given the opportunity to share its response to the community question.* ➤

(P) Does the value of good work "in-form" your heart in a way that influences your conscious actions? Explain.

(C) Is there a type of good work by which we, as a school community, are known?

## Reorientation

*Answer the personal (P) questions and, if in a group situation, the community (C) questions. The facilitator will have each group report back to the main group. The facilitator may record the responses to the community (C) questions and work toward a communal discernment of a praxis to which all are willing to make a commitment.*

(P) What is the type of good work that you do in the world? Is it time for you to either recommit yourself to this good work or reorient yourself in the direction of a new good work? How would you do this?

(C) Is it time to recommit or reorient ourselves with renewed vigour to building a particular praxis (faith-in-action) that animates the school with the virtue of faith? How could we do this?

# 2. THE SPLENDOROUS FLOWER

*If you have not previously reflected on the description of faith given at the beginning of this section, follow the directions at the start of Reflection #1: The Christmas Miracle. If you have already used the description of faith, then either reflect on the earlier definitions (if posted or recollected) or take a moment to record your current definition of faith (your understanding could have changed or grown since the last session). If in a group, take time to share the definitions. In the interest of activating prior learning, have each group come up with a definition of faith and share it with the large group or revisit the definition given during Reflection #1.*

*Read the scripture passage below, individually or as a group.*

> They came to Jericho. As he and his disciples and a large crowd were leaving Jericho, Bartimaeus son of Timaeus, a blind beggar, was sitting by the roadside. When he heard that it was Jesus of Nazareth, he began to shout out and say, "Jesus, Son of David, have mercy on me!" Many sternly ordered him to be quiet, but he cried out even more loudly, "Son of David, have mercy on me!" Jesus stood still and said, "Call him here." And they called the blind man, saying to him, "Take heart; get up, he is calling you." So throwing off his cloak, he sprang up and came to Jesus. Then Jesus said to him, "What do you want me to do for you?" The blind man said to him, "My teacher, let me see again." Jesus said to him, "Go; your faith has made you well." Immediately he regained his sight and followed him on the way. (Mark 10:46-52)

*Reconsider your definition of faith (your personal one or the group definition). Is there anything you would change? Allow time for discussion and ask for feedback to the large group.*

*Read the story below, individually or as a group.*

One morning, after doing bus greeting, I turned to walk back to the front door of the school. Then I heard my name being called. I turned around and saw the corpulent outline of one of our Grade 1 students running as fast as his feet could carry him, screaming, "Mr. Laxton! Mr. Laxton!" I wondered what was wrong, as his little world had been coming apart as of late (his parents had separated). There he was, bounding down the sidewalk, his cheeks flushed by the exertion; there was a radiance about him. I wondered what he was going to ask me and how I might respond. My heart was heavy and I was expecting the worst.

When he caught up to me, he looked up with the innocence and purity that is really only possible in childhood and said, "I wanted to give you this." He handed me a beautiful but wilted flower he had picked that morning on his way to school. (I could only imagine which of the neighbours' gardens it may have come from.) I didn't miss the metaphor in the occasion and thought that he, too, was just as surely wilting, but his was from the growing emotional desert of his circumstances. Nonetheless, his face still projected all the beauty of a splendorous flower. He reminded me of the beauty of faith, when we have complete trust in the benevolent goodness of the Creator. Unfortunately, we can be so blinded by the cloak of current circumstance, that we can't see the radiant splendour of a God whose love transcends the world in a way that exceeds the surpassing beauty of a flower. I also thought of all the school staff who support students with drooping spirits due to the vicissitudes of their fledgling lives. You are the benevolent stewards that rain the waters of renewed life on the flowers that thirst – waters that formed an eternal fount on the day of your baptism. God bless us all.

*Reflect on the story:*

Does the story strike a chord with your experience? If so, try to identify not only the chord, but also the underlying value. If not, does it strike a note of discord? If so, why?

- *If you are in a group situation, allow time for group feedback on a voluntary basis.*

- *If you are doing this on your own, journal your thoughts for later reflection.*

## ENCULTURATING CATHOLIC CHARACTER

### Experience

*Write a personal response to the statement below. If in a group, share the story with the group. Each group may select one story to share with the large group. Don't reveal the identity of the person(s) in the story.*

Share a story of an encounter you had with a student in which your faith played a significant role in your response to the situation.

### Understanding

*Answer either or both of the questions below. If in a group, share your responses with the group. Have each group share one response with the large group.*

Put into your own words the meaning of the statement that "you are the benevolent stewards that rain the waters of renewed life on the flowers that thirst – waters that formed an eternal fount on the day of your baptism." What is the "fount" of your faith?

➤

## Reflection

*Write your response to the personal (P) question below. If in a group, on a voluntary basis, share your response with the group. Groups may, on a voluntary basis, share a story with the large group. The facilitator may skip the personal question and move to the community (C) question. Each group should be given the opportunity to share its response to the community question.*

(P) On a personal level, can you identify the "cloak" (bias, circumstance, life events, etc.) that limits you from having a more intimate experience of faith?

(C) What is the "cloak" that we as a community must remove in order to not only come to Jesus ourselves, but to lead others to Jesus as well?

## Reorientation

*Answer the personal (P) question and, if in a group situation, the community (C) questions. The facilitator will have each group report back to the large group. The facilitator may record the responses to the community questions and work toward a communal discernment of a praxis to which all are willing to make a commitment.*

(P) In the light of your dispensing with your figurative cloak, what is it that your faith is "springing up" to (values, virtues, etc.)?

(C) What is it that our faith community is "springing up" to at this moment in time? How can we use this dynamism to build a stronger faith community?

# 3. FIRST HOLY COMMUNION

*If you have not previously reflected on the description of faith given at the beginning of this section, follow the directions at the start of Reflection #1: The Christmas Miracle. If you have previously used the description of faith, then take a moment to record your current understanding of faith. If in a group, take time to share the definitions in your group. In the interest of activating prior learning, have each group come up with a definition of faith and share it with the large group, or revisit the definition given during previous reflections.*

*Read the scripture passage (below), individually or as a group.*

> **There is one body and one Spirit, just as you were called to the one hope of our calling, one Lord, one faith, one baptism, one God and Father of all, who is above all and through all and in all. (Ephesians 4:4-6)**

*Reconsider your personal or group definition of faith. Is there anything you would change? Allow time for discussion and ask for feedback to the large group.*

*Read the story below (individually or as a group).*

First Holy Communion: how well that phrase captures the richness and beauty of our faith!

On one level it speaks of a "First," which is a promise that many more are to come. If there's one inexhaustible quality in life, it is that of the promise it holds. Life without promise is life without depth.

Second, the whole notion of something being "Holy" is more than rhetorical: it speaks to our engagement with life in a way that is much more than profane. All life is suffused with holiness, but how often do we reflect on its meaning? I suppose we could consult the "experts," but I prefer to consult life: a child's picture of God; the first time you held your baby; the tears shed in the solitude of your heart for the child who doesn't know enough to cry; the first spring crocus; the last leaf falling in autumn; the last time you said "I love you" to someone dear to you.

Finally, there is the promise of "Communion." The story of Adam and Eve is really the story of a loss of communion, which became the legacy of all who were to be called human. It is a mixed blessing that we are given: to be able to understand what communion is and to know that we have been separated from it. There are many religious moments in our lives – both the ordinary and the extraordinary kind – that restore a state of communion. The ordinary are those events that I call holy, in the sense used above, and the extraordinary are those of the sacramental kind, when the children in our care are brought into the embrace of all that is worth holding onto, so that they, too, may realize that the promise of faith is fulfilled in the ultimate act of letting go.

*Reflect on the story:*

Does the story strike a chord with your experience? If so, try to identify not only the chord, but also the underlying value. If not, does it strike a note of discord? If so, why?

- *If you are in a group situation, allow time for group feedback on a voluntary basis.*
- *If you are doing this on your own, journal your thoughts for later reflection.*

## ENCULTURATING CATHOLIC CHARACTER

### Experience

*Write your response to the statement below. If in a group, share your response with the group. Have each group share one story with the large group.*

Share the story of your First Holy Communion.

## Understanding

*Write your response to the question below. If in a group, share your response with the group. Have each group share one response with the large group.*

What is the faith that you give witness to in your daily encounters with children? If you say God, what image of God do you use (e.g., Creator, Redeemer, Holy Spirit, Judge, Counsellor)?

## Reflection

*Write your response to the personal (P) question below. If in a group, on a voluntary basis, share your response with the group. Groups may, on a voluntary basis, share a story with the large group. The facilitator may skip the personal question and move to the community (C) question. Each group should be given the opportunity to share its response to the community question.*

(P) Where is your place of holy communion?

(C) Where is our collective place of holy communion?

## Reorientation

*Answer the personal (P) question and, if in a group, the community (C) question. The facilitator will have each group report back to the main group. The facilitator may record the responses to the question and work toward a communal discernment of a praxis to which all are willing to make a commitment.*

(P) Into whose lives do you bring a sense of holy communion? How?

(C) What rituals or practices can we build into our school praxis to make each day one of holy communion?

# 4. THE CANVAS OF THE SOUL

*If you have not previously reflected on the description of faith given at the beginning of this section, follow the directions at the start of Reflection #1: The Christmas Miracle. If you have already used the description of faith, then take a moment to record your current understanding of faith. If in a group, take time to share the definitions in your group. In the interest of activating prior learning, have each group come up with a definition of faith and share it with the large group, or revisit the definition given during previous reflections.*

*Read the scripture passage (below), individually or as a group.*

> **For I am longing to see you so that I may share with you some spiritual gift to strengthen you – or rather so that we may be mutually encouraged by each other's faith, both yours and mine. (Romans 1:11-12)**

*Reconsider your definition of faith (your personal one or, if in a group, the group definition). Is there anything you would change? Allow time for discussion and ask for feedback to the large group.*

*Read the story below, individually or as a group.*

I like to use the metaphor of an artist's canvas for the image of the soul. I've imagined that when we pass on to the next life and arrive at the "gates of Heaven," we will be required to unveil our canvas for inspection by St. Peter. I have always hoped that if this was the case, that on the canvas of each of my students' souls there would be one brushstroke that I may have contributed to the landscape of their spiritual life. Perhaps, of even more significance, I hope that when I look at my own canvas, I will see a self-portrait composed of myriad brushstrokes made by my students. If that were true, then my portrait would be have been formed by my community of faith. I didn't realize that when I arrived at our school, I was coming to a school of artists; there is no doubt that each person there has contributed to the canvases of the souls of our students. I know that because I've caught them painting on mine.

*Reflect on the story:*

Does the story strike a chord with your experience? If so, try to identify not only the chord, but also the underlying value. If not, does it strike a note of discord? If so, why?

- *If you are in a group situation, allow time for group feedback on a voluntary basis.*

- *If you are doing this on your own, journal your thoughts for later reflection.*

## ENCULTURATING CATHOLIC CHARACTER

### Experience

*Write your response to the statement below. If in a group, share your response with the group. Have each group share one story with the large group.*

Recount a time when you knew that the work you were doing was "soulful."

### Understanding

*Write your response to the question below. If in a group, share your response with the group. Have each group share one story with the large group.*

What is your understanding of the connection between "spiritual gifts" and "faith"? ➤

## Reflection

*Write your response to the personal (P) question below. If in a group, on a voluntary basis, share your response with the group. Groups may, on a voluntary basis, share a story with the large group. The facilitator may skip the personal question and move to the community (C) question. Each group should be given the opportunity to share its response to the community question.*

(P) What is one artistic image that would capture the spiritual giftedness of your soul?

(C) What is one artistic image that would capture the spiritual giftedness of our school?

## Reorientation

*Answer the personal (P) question and, if in a group situation, the community (C) question. The facilitator will have each group report back to the main group. The facilitator may record the responses to the questions and work toward a communal discernment of a praxis to which all are willing to make a commitment.*

(P) How could you use the artistic image of your soul as a compass to direct your way of being in the world?

(C) What could we do to engage all the members of our community in building a culture of soulful artisans?

# II. HOPE

*Please follow the methodology outlined under the particular virtue of faith (or see the section entitled Methodology at the end of the book).*

It has been my experience that the overwhelming majority of those who choose to work in Catholic schools are persons of hope. On the most fundamental level we are motivated by our love for children. Children can be God's tiny agents calling forth love from the depths of our being. We are not often conscious of the depth of love within our hearts and souls; yet, it spontaneously bursts forth in response to the needs of the children in our care. On another level, we are also motivated by a sense of hope, and all hope is ultimately rooted in the resurrection. The passion, death and resurrection of Jesus bear testament to the truth of the virtues of faith, hope and love. The very structure of our being, with its desire to know and love God, engenders a transcendent sense of hope, one that leads us on a path to salvation. Each of the stories that follow illustrates the hope inherent in the concreteness of life, which is underwritten by a transcendent sense of the hope of resurrection and the love of God.

# 5. "FREE WILLY"

Then [the sailors] said to [Jonah], "What shall we do to you, that the sea may quieten down for us?" For the sea was growing more and more tempestuous. He said to them, "Pick me up and throw me into the sea; then the sea will quieten down for you; for I know it is because of me that this great storm has come upon you." Nevertheless, the men rowed hard to bring the ship back to land, but they could not, for the sea grew more and more stormy against them. Then they cried out to the Lord, "Please, O Lord, we pray, do not let us perish on account of this man's life. Do not make us guilty of innocent blood; for you, O Lord, have done as it pleased you." So they picked Jonah up and threw him into the sea; and the sea ceased from its raging. Then the men feared the Lord even more, and they offered a sacrifice to the Lord and made vows. But the Lord provided a large fish to swallow up Jonah; and Jonah was in the belly of the fish for three days and three nights. Then the Lord spoke to the fish, and it spewed Jonah out upon the dry land. The word of the Lord came to Jonah a second time, saying, "Get up, go to Nineveh, that great city, and proclaim to it the message that I tell you." So Jonah set out and went to Nineveh, according to the word of the Lord. (Jonah 1:11-17; 2:10; 3:1-3)

I ventured into the laboratory of our Grade 7 class the other day to observe the workings of our most industrious students' minds. They were devising mechanical levers, gears and other fanciful devices to lift an imaginary whale in a heavenly direction for purposes that I'm sure were most humane. These devices, which were intended to "Free Willy" of any hazardous aquatic circumstance, also liberated the most holy of human dynamisms: the inquiring mind. It seems that the outer universe we gaze upon is mirrored by the inner universe of our minds. What a blessing it is that we have the ability not only to pose questions, but to successfully seek the answers. It has been said that "all roads lead to Rome"; the same may be said of the hope of our spiritual quests, in which all questions (ultimately) lead to God. Jonah's heroic journey began in the belly of a fish (or what some believe to be a whale). In mythological terms, this may very well have represented the "dark night of the soul" in his journey to self-enlightenment. For our budding scientists, who knows where their quests may lead their souls? I know, for now at least, that thanks to their teacher, their journey is being carried out in the bowels of our school, from where I trust our students will emerge enlightened and proclaiming God's message of hope.

## ENCULTURATING CATHOLIC CHARACTER

### Experience

Recount a story of someone whose unquenchable desire to find the answers to their questions inspired you.

### Understanding

What is the nature of the connection between asking questions and coming to affirm the presence of God?

### Reflection

(P) Describe the dynamism, within yourself, that seeks answers to questions about God.

(C) Do we, as a community, have a dynamic spirit that not only poses questions, but seeks the answers to those questions?

### Reorientation

(P) What are the key questions you seek the answers to in life? What do the questions you ask tell you about your journey?

(C) What are the key questions that we, as a school community, are posing and collectively seeking the answers to?

# 6. THE IRIDESCENT SPRING PEACOCK

**So we have the prophetic message more fully confirmed. You will do well to be attentive to this as to a lamp shining in a dark place, until the day dawns and the morning star rises in your hearts. (2 Peter 1:19)**

Can you imagine my surprise when our new girl, who couldn't write her name at the beginning of the year and was painfully lagging behind the rest of her peers, showed up on my doorstep and wanted to read me a sentence she had written? We all know this child, the one who can stare vacantly at a page and only occasionally scratch symbols that are more expressive of internal frustration than the joy of writing. The chasm between sensate experience and articulated thought seems unbridgeable.

Well, you can't imagine (or maybe you can) the pride with which she read her sentence. Not even the most majestic iridescent spring peacock could match the beauty of her proclamation. Her newfound ability was the wind beneath her wings. It was as if each word that she came to master had a breath of its own that pushed the quills of her soul's imagination higher and higher into the heights of holiness, where words are animated by the spirit of life. Surely the "morning star" was rising in her heart and a new day was dawning. This little girl is our own sacred version of the "flesh made word." Salutation to all whose primary vocation is to primp and preen the quills of both pen and soul.

## ENCULTURATING CATHOLIC CHARACTER

### Experience

Recount a time when you really experienced the power of the word.

### Understanding

Why is the prophetic word a powerful source of hope (a star rising in your heart)?

### Reflection

(P) What are the five most powerful words of your prophetic heart?

(C) What are the five most powerful words of our collective prophetic heart?

### Reorientation

(P) Which words are most prominent in your daily interactions? Do they reflect a sense of hope?

(C) What are the words of hope upon which we can build up our community? How can we achieve this?

# 7. "HI"

**May the God of hope fill you with all joy and peace in believing, so that you may abound in hope by the power of the Holy Spirit. (Romans 15:13)**

This past week, something really remarkable happened. A young boy said "Hi" to me. In and of itself, that might seem rather unremarkable, but when you consider that at the beginning of the year this young lad had to be coaxed into even looking at me, then coached into making an inaudible sound that would pass for "Hi," it was quite astonishing. The sheer joy that I felt (and I know he is feeling, as are all those who believed in him) when, in an unsolicited and spontaneous way, he cracked that chasm of silence and filled the air with a resounding pronouncement of his passage into the world of articulation, is a thing of wonder. It reminded me of how we, in our very humble and unpretentious way, witness the "good news" and affect our own form of healing. We must always remember that by following the way of Christ, we, too, ascend the mountain of our innate spiritual potential and see the world from a new vantage point. Thanks to all those who helped him (teachers, educational assistants, secretary and custodian), our own little miracle child now says "Hi" and "Bye" and can pronounce his own name.

## ENCULTURATING CATHOLIC CHARACTER

### Experience

Recount an occasion when you helped someone give voice to what had kept them mute.

### Understanding

What is it in your life that speaks with the voice of hope?

### Reflection

(P) In what way is your sense of hope grounded in feelings of "joy and peace"?

(C) Do we as a community have a sense of hope that is grounded in feelings of "joy and peace"?

### Reorientation

(P) In what ways do you communicate hope to the children you work with?

(C) In what ways does our school community witness hope? What commitment do we need to make to reaffirm our sense of hope or to build a new vision of hope?

# 8. RITES OF PASSAGE

**… so that, with the eyes of your heart enlightened, you may know what is the hope to which he has called you, what are the riches of his glorious inheritance among the saints… (Ephesians 1:18)**

In this year's chapter in the annals of our school, a very important occasion occurred on Thursday of this past week. For most of us, it probably passed unnoticed amid the near cyclonic forces of events that spin throughout the day, but for those with the eyes of their heart enlightened, a threshold was surmounted. This threshold may seem trivial to the foolish, but for those who have the wisdom of the sages, it was an event worthy of communal celebration. You may have noticed the swish of air fanned by the windmill of frenzied activity. You may have heard the roar of team victory, paramount to that of an Olympic team that has just won the gold medal. You may have heard the sigh of relief of an exhausted teacher, who has just negotiated her students through one of the gruelling rites of passage. She is invested, once again, with a sense of hope and pride in her young artisans, who have left behind a small vestige of childhood.

The occasion to which I'm referring is that momentous day when all the Junior Kindergarten students don their own coats without the divine intervention of the teacher's hand. Putting on one's apparel is a sure sign of the awakening of a sense of self, a trait that is much needed to survive in this world. It is difficult to weigh the effect of such an occasion on the conscious minds of our youngest students. Somewhere down in the depths of their psyches, there has been laid a cornerstone in the foundation of their own self-conception and a new confidence in their ability to master the challenges of life. Congratulations to all involved!

## ENCULTURATING CATHOLIC CHARACTER

### Experience

Recount a time when you realized that you were involved in a spiritual rite of passage.

### Understanding

What was it about this experience that made it a spiritual passage?

### Reflection

(P) Have you ever felt that with "heart enlightened" you can see the hope of your calling? Explain.

(C) Do we have a communal sense of having a "heart enlightened" by the hope of our calling? What is that sense of hope grounded in?

### Reorientation

(P) Which of your rites of passage were most significant in your life? What role did hope play in the passage?

(C) What are the significant rites of passage that we celebrate in our school? How can we build them into celebrations of hope?

# III. LOVE

*Please follow the methodology outlined under the particular virtue of faith (or see the section entitled Methodology at the end of the book).*

What would we be without love? We certainly wouldn't be fully human. Love is probably the closest experience we can have of God. The desire to be loved and to love grounds us in love's immanence, as realized in the concreteness of life. Love, however, is self-transcending in its search for its ultimate source, which is God. The following stories illustrate the importance of an orientation of love in the life of the community.

# 9. MYSTERY, MIRACLE AND LOSS

For men are not cast off by the Lord forever. Though he brings grief, he will show compassion, so great is his unfailing love. For he does not willingly bring affliction or grief to the children of men. (Lamentations 3:31)

It has been said that from the moment of birth, we experience loss. The first loss is of the intra-uterine sanctum, that most sacred of places, where the mystery of the cosmos meets the miracle of the womb. Mystery, miracle and loss weave a pattern of destiny into the fabric of our lives. The cosmos would not exist without mystery; life would not exist without miracle; meaning would not exist without loss. This week we suffered a loss when one of our special students left our community. Those who viewed him from "without" and with eyes not fully open might fixate on his spontaneous and seemingly incoherent outbursts or the repetitive gyrations of his body. Those who knew him from "within" saw that he was God's gift to this community, reminding us of the sheer exuberance of life and calling forth love from all those he encountered. In many ways he was our prophet, speaking God's message of love and joy. We feel a sense of loss with his departure and yet, even in our loss, he has gifted us with the fullness of life. He has left us with a renewed sense of purpose and an increased capacity for love. He has made this community a more loving place to be.

## ENCULTURATING CATHOLIC CHARACTER

### Experience

Recount a time when the loss of a student really impacted your school community.

### Understanding

Why did the loss of that student impact the school so much?

### Reflection

(P) Which of the following are most "in-formative" in your spiritual life: mystery, miracle or loss? Why?

(C) What role do mystery, miracle and loss play in the life of our community?

### Reorientation

(P) In what ways do you reach out to the students who are suffering from loss?

(C) How can we build a commitment to love the lost children in our care?

# 10. EA

> But Moses said to the Lord, "O my Lord, I have never been eloquent, neither in the past nor even now that you have spoken to your servant; but I am slow of speech and slow of tongue." Then the Lord said to him, "Who gives speech to mortals? Who makes them mute or deaf, seeing or blind? Is it not I, the Lord? Now go, and I will be with your mouth and teach you what you are to speak." But he said, "O my Lord, please send someone else." Then the anger of the Lord was kindled against Moses and he said, "What of your brother Aaron, the Levite? I know that he can speak fluently; even now he is coming out to meet you, and when he sees you his heart will be glad. You shall speak to him and put the words in his mouth; and I will be with your mouth and with his mouth, and will teach you what you shall do. He indeed shall speak for you to the people; he shall serve as a mouth for you, and you shall serve as God for him. Take in your hand this staff, with which you shall perform the signs." (Exodus 4:10-17)

The designation "educational assistant" hardly seems to capture either the loving presence of the person or the sacredness of the vocation. Perhaps "educational Aaronite," in the tradition of Aaron, is a more appropriate title for the acronym "EA." Aaron, as Moses' assistant, went on to advocate for Moses and assist him until Moses gained enough confidence to speak for himself and to work miracles. It was from the lineage of Aaron that an important line of priests descended. "Educational Aaronites" should recognize that they, too, are working in unison with God, as spiritual sisters and brothers to our children who, through a lack of confidence, may avoid the call from God, just as Moses did.

I can't imagine a holier vocation than helping to give children the confidence to be all that God called them to be. Our EAs surely awaken the voice of God in our special students, for I have seen the signs that they have performed: children reading and reciting, for whom the world of text was a foreign land, as was Egypt for the Israelites.

## ENCULTURATING CATHOLIC CHARACTER

### Experience

Recount an occasion where you witnessed someone acting as an "educational Aaronite."

### Understanding

What was it about that person that made you think he/she was acting on behalf of God?

### Reflection

(P) Have you ever felt you were being called to speak on God's behalf? Describe the feeling.

(C) What is it that our community is being called to say, on behalf of those with no voice, at this moment in time?

### Reorientation

(P) What will help you overcome your hesitation to speak on behalf of God?

(C) What commitment can we build, as a community, to become "educational Aaronites" in order to speak on behalf of those who have no voice?

# 11. THE GENTLE GATHERER

**"Come to me, all you that are weary and are carrying heavy burdens, and I will give you rest. Take my yoke upon you, and learn from me; for I am gentle and humble in heart, and you will find rest for your souls." (Matthew 11:28-29)**

Deep within the sanctum of our school, there is a sanctuary that only those who toil on its holy ground know. It is the Chapel of the Gatherer, otherwise known as the special education room. This is the sacred space of the lay apostolate of our gentle gatherer. To be a shepherd is to be a gatherer in the manner of Jesus, who left the flock to gather in the lost sheep. Our gentle gatherer does the same.

One of the first images we encounter in the Hebrew Scriptures is that of God establishing order over chaos; that has been the mission of our gentle gatherer. She collects those souls who are lost in the chaos of their lives and establishes an order that is anchored in love, acceptance and attachment. She knows better than most that unless the intellectual growth of a child is situated within a matrix of emotional, psychological, social and spiritual order, then chaos reigns. If you were to look into her eyes at this very moment, you would see that they are welling up with tears. Let there be no mistake: those tears are not for herself, but for the children she gathers and whose thirst she quenches from the wells of her humanity – wells whose source lies in her faith in Jesus the redeemer. On behalf of all of those who have sought the solace of the Chapel, we thank you and honour you, our gentle gatherer.

## ENCULTURATING CATHOLIC CHARACTER

### Experience

Can you recall a time when you were "gathered in" by the arms of someone in love and support?

### Understanding

In what way(s) did this embrace reveal the "gentle and humble in heart"?

### Reflection

(P) To what extent was this experience of being "gathered in" a spiritual one for you? Why?

(C) Who are the children in our community who need to be "gathered in" to find rest for their souls?

### Reorientation

(P) What change do you need to make to effect a ministry of gathering for the children in your care?

(C) How can we build a praxis of gathering into our community?

# 12. "I LOVE YOU"

Now the festival of Unleavened Bread, which is called the
Passover, was near. The chief priests and the scribes were
looking for a way to put Jesus to death, for they were afraid
of the people. Then Satan entered into Judas called Iscariot,
who was one of the twelve; he went away and conferred with
the chief priests and officers of the temple police about how
he might betray him to them. They were greatly pleased
and agreed to give him money. So he consented and began
to look for an opportunity to betray him to them.... While
he was still speaking, suddenly a crowd came, and the one
called Judas, one of the twelve, was leading them. He approached Jesus to kiss him; but Jesus said to him, "Judas,
is it with a kiss that you are betraying the Son of Man?"
(Luke 22:1-6, 47-48)

I have always been puzzled and saddened by the betrayal of Jesus
by Judas. How could someone so close to Jesus not be enveloped
by his love? Did Judas love only Jesus' divinity and reject his humanity? Luke's gospel account of Judas's betrayal is unique from the
accounts in Matthew and Mark, as Luke notes the power of Satan in
the downfall of Judas.

This raises some interesting questions for me. Why did Jesus not
exorcize the demon from Judas as he had done for others? Was it all
part of the unfolding of God's plan? Luke's gospel has some important messages for a staff that is dedicated to the formation of young
people. One pervasive motif in this gospel is Jesus' healing by casting out demons. Last week, one of our teachers, who has been most
patient and understanding with one of our little boys who faces his
own challenges, was quite surprised when the little fellow suddenly
gave her a hug and said, "I love you." For this little fellow, betrayal
came in the form of a demon (Fetal Alcohol Syndrome) that seized
him in the very womb of sacredness. The demon seized the very
epicentre of his development and distorted its growth by wreaking
intellectual, emotional and physical damage. The human condition

is one that is intimately tied to the organic structure of being, but it also transcends mere corporality to reveal its fullest manifestation in the ethereal realm of the spiritual. This child's spirit is the buoyant force in a life that is weighted down by his biological and psychic afflictions. For our little fellow, even in the midst of turmoil, there is a healing of sorts going on – one that is being mediated through the love of the teacher and acknowledged in his declaration to her: "I love you."

## ENCULTURATING CATHOLIC CHARACTER

### Experience

Recount a time when someone's spirit was the buoy that lifted that person above their circumstance.

### Understanding

What was it about their spirituality that provided the buoyant force in their life?

### Reflection

(P) What role does love play in the buoyancy of your spirit?

(C) What is it that gives buoyancy to our communal spirit?

### Reorientation

(P) What steps do you need to take to allow the spirit of love to be a more buoyant force in your life?

(C) How can we, as a school community, build students up in order to help them overcome the betrayals in their lives?

# THE CARDINAL VIRTUES

*Read the definition (to yourself or as a group) of the cardinal virtues to provide an overall context for the particular virtue.*

While the graces of faith, hope and love are operative in the sense that they come from above, the cardinal virtues reveal the workings of a grace that invites our cooperation. The cardinal virtues are those that allow us to build up our own constitution through discernment of moral truth and commitment to doing the right thing.

# I. FORTITUDE

*Begin by writing your own definition of the particular virtue in question.*

*Then read the description below (to yourself or as a group) before exploring any of the reflections under this particular virtue.*

The particular virtue of fortitude is associated with courage. Showing courage in a given situation is not an exact science. Certainly Socrates had the courage of his convictions, being put to death for his uncompromising search for truth. Just as certainly, Jesus had the courage to live up to his prophetic calling. Sometimes heroes are described as having courage when, in a spontaneous gesture, they plunge headfirst into a perilous situation. The hero often says that she or he didn't have time to think, but just reacted. I want to reflect on a different type of courage: one that some of our students and staff have. For a number of our students, it takes a lot of courage to come to school and face the humiliation of being lapped in the academic race or being left behind in their social circumstance. For our staff, it takes courage to lay down their lives in the form of a vocation. The following stories explore the courage of these students and staff.

*Now reconsider your definition of "fortitude": Is there anything you would change? If you are facilitating a group situation, allow time for participants to share their definitions in small groups. Ask the groups to come up with a definition of fortitude and then share it with the large group. Invite the groups to record their definitions for posting in a "Virtues" corner.*

# 13. THIS MOMENT OF LUMINOSITY

*Read the scripture quote.*

> "I hereby command you: Be strong and courageous; do not
> be frightened or dismayed, for the Lord your God is with
> you wherever you go." (Joshua 1:9)

*Reconsider your most recent definition of the particular virtue. Is there
anything you would change? Groups: Allow time for discussion and
feedback to the large group. Individuals: Journal your response.*

*Read the story.*

Have you ever been camping in the middle of a forest and wher-
ever you look you see nothing but darkness, then suddenly,
without fanfare or expectation, a beam of light cuts through the
darkness and illuminates the otherwise hidden recesses of the inner
arboreal sanctum? What you see before your eyes are majestic sil-
houettes that stand veiled in the train of the full moon, as if exposed
for the first time to human eyes.

That is similar to my experience this week when one of our
wounded children burst into the office asking to see me in a tone of
voice that was more excited than troubled. Proudly, he crossed the
well-trodden threshold of my office, but his feet were light, as if his
broken spirit had suddenly sprouted wings to carry him to places
he had seldom been. "Look!" he said, as he showed me a picture of
a bear, carefully coloured according to a mathematical legend that
mapped out a chromatic scheme amid the chaotic pieces of a puzzle
that hid its image. "What a beautiful picture!" I said. "Look, you've
coloured all the parts correctly." He stood there, as if basking in the
glory of his accomplishment, when I added, "I always knew you
were a smart boy." That's when it happened. Quite unexpectedly and
without fanfare, a smile broke across his face and his entire persona
radiated with the silhouette of the beautiful child who is often hidden in the recesses of his own inner sanctum. It was the first time

I had seen him smile all year (it was near the end of June) and his grin quickened my heart and lifted my spirit. I cannot take credit for this moment of luminosity, for there are many others who deserve the credit, especially those who have given so much of themselves to him. We live in a profoundly mysterious universe; largely due to the efforts of courageous people like them, the universe has a heart that pulses with compassion and a spirit that seeks the eternal.

*Reflect on the story:*

Does the story strike a chord with your experience? If so, try to identify not only the chord, but also the underlying value. If not, does it strike a note of discord? If so, why?

- *If you are in a group situation, allow time for group feedback on a voluntary basis.*
- *If you are doing this on your own, journal your thoughts for later reflection.*

## ENCULTURATING CATHOLIC CULTURE

### Experience

*Write your response to the question below. If in a group, share your response with the group. Each group will select one story to share with the large group.*

Can you recall an experience of sudden illumination, where what seemed hidden suddenly burst forth from the darkness to become known?

### Understanding

*Write your response to the question below. If in a group, on a voluntary basis, share your response with the group. Have each group, on a voluntary basis, share one response with the large group.*

How can the experience of illumination be related to courage?

## Reflection

*Write your response to the personal (P) question given under "Reflection." If in a group, on a voluntary basis, share your response with the group. Groups may, on a voluntary basis, share a story with the large group. The facilitator may skip the personal question and move to the community (C) question. Each group should be given the opportunity to share their response to the community question.*

(P) Insights (sudden moments of illumination) also apply to the affective domain of feelings and values. Have you ever had a moment of illumination when your feelings have led you to understanding of the meaning of a value (such as courage or forgiveness)?

(C) In what ways does Christ illuminate our communal spirit?

## Reorientation

*Answer the personal (P) questions and if in a group situation, the community (C) question. The facilitator will have each group report back to the main group. The facilitator may record the responses to the community (C) question and work toward a communal discernment of a praxis to which all are willing to make a commitment.*

(P) In what way was "the Lord your God" with you in your moment of illumination?

(C) How can we build an academic program that couples the demands for cognitive growth with the need for spiritual illumination?

# 14. THE BREATH OF LIFE

**When the day of Pentecost had come, they were all together in one place. And suddenly from heaven there came a sound like the rush of a violent wind, and it filled the entire house where they were sitting. Divided tongues, as of fire, appeared among them, and a tongue rested on each of them. All of them were filled with the Holy Spirit and began to speak in other languages, as the Spirit gave them ability. Now there were devout Jews from every nation under heaven living in Jerusalem. And at this sound the crowd gathered and was bewildered, because each one heard them speaking in the native language of each. Amazed and astonished, they asked, "Are not all these who are speaking Galileans? And how is it that we hear, each of us, in our own native language?" (Acts 2:1-8)**

There is a wonderful story in Genesis whereupon God formed humankind: "[T]hen the Lord God formed man from the dust of the ground, and breathed into his nostrils the breath of life; and the man became a living being" (Genesis 2:7). *Ruach* is the Hebrew word for "wind," but it can also mean "breath" or "spirit." In an etymological sense, breath, soul and spirit are one at their root. The ancient people realized that life was miraculous; life begins with the first breath (they had no scientific knowledge of conception); and life ends with the last breath. Who else could be behind such a vital force in life other than God?

Who can forget the first breath their newborn child takes and the resounding "cry of being" that follows? Who can forget the final breath a loved one takes and the resounding "cry of silence"? In both the cry of being and the cry of silence, God is present to either deliver or receive. However, sometimes God needs a little help, such as when things go awry. That was the case this week when one of our own little lambs was struck with the venomous bite of anaphylaxis. Our own guardian angels became incarnate in the form of extraordinary people who walk in humble ways. While this child was enveloped in the early onset of this serpentine constriction of her vital passageway, the angels were already in action. One immediately diagnosed the problem, another grasped her in the gentle but Herculean grip of life that refused to let her slip away, another was the quiet voice of reason, another called 9-1-1; I administered the EpiPen while this young girl struggled to avoid the very lance of her liberation. This holy gathering was the antidote to the serpentine poison. We wouldn't let the breath of life be extinguished. Because of our actions, this little seraph will live to breathe another day – one in which breath, soul and spirit dance to the miracle of life.

## ENCULTURATING CATHOLIC CHARACTER

### Experience

Have you ever had the experience of seeing a baby gasp for their first breath of air or a loved one who has breathed their last? If so, describe the feelings associated with the occasion.

### Understanding

Scripture speaks of God breathing life into creation and Jesus breathing the life of the Holy Spirit into his disciples. In what ways was the Spirit present in your experience?

### Reflection

(P) Have you ever felt that the Holy Spirit had filled you with the courage of your convictions? What change did that bring about in you?

(C) The notion of divided tongues can be seen, metaphorically, as a blessing (Holy Spirit) or a curse (snake). How can we make sure it is a blessing in our community?  ➤

### Reorientation

(P) The apostles were hidden in a room for fear of what was unfolding in the world. Which room do you shut yourself in? What is it that you fear? How can you develop the courage to open the windows of your soul to the breath of the Spirit?

(C) Students often perceive us as speaking in tongues (different grades/subjects). How can we help them see that these tongues are but manifestations of the same Spirit that descended as separate tongues of fire at Pentecost?

# 15. INSPIRATION

> Jesus said to them again, "Peace be with you. As the Father has sent me, so I send you." When he had said this, he breathed on them and said to them, "Receive the Holy Spirit." (John 20:21-22)

I was working at my desk when our benevolent secretary said, "There's someone here to see you Mr. Laxton." As I pivoted in my chair to see who was coming, I was met with the embrace of an eight-year-old child. Now this hug was a special one, because it enveloped not only my neck, but my heart as well. It was our beloved little lamb coming back in to say "Hi" after her long struggle with anaphylaxis and the resulting lung collapse and asthmatic reaction. My exuberance was tempered by the laboured breathing that her angelic aura almost completely masked. Here, in this little miracle of being, was the confluence of the many meanings of inspiration: it can represent the presence of the divine in a sacred moment of revelation, as illustrated by the biblical image of God breathing life into the nostrils of Adam, or Jesus breathing the Holy Spirit into the lives of the disciples. I believe we had our sacred moment as she clung to life amid the massive assault of her own body's immune response to a supposed alien invader. Inspiration can also mean the seemingly simple act of moving air into the lungs, something that even now, for her, is a gift, because her body's misinformed memory seeks to fight phantom ghosts. Finally, it could be defined as the act of influencing others. I know that I won't ever look at her the same way again; I will always see the little girl who had the courage to slay the Goliath of her own viscera. In that way she is an inspiration for me to face the Goliaths of my own life.

## ENCULTURATING CATHOLIC CHARACTER

### Experience

Think of a story of courage that inspired you.

### Understanding

What was it that was so inspirational?

### Reflection

(P) We often look for inspirational moments, but most types of inspiration are in the form of a lifelong ethos dedicated to a specific value or set of values (a virtuous person). What are the values that guide your inspirational story?

(C) What is the inspirational message of our community?

### Reorientation

(P) How can you open yourself up to receive the breath of the Holy Spirit?

(C) How can we build a community ethos of courageous inspiration?

# 16. PASTOR OF THE PASTURE

"Very truly, I tell you, anyone who does not enter the sheep-fold by the gate but climbs in by another way is a thief and a bandit. The one who enters by the gate is the shepherd of the sheep. The gatekeeper opens the gate for him, and the sheep hear his voice. He calls his own sheep by name and leads them out. When he has brought out all his own, he goes ahead of them, and the sheep follow him because they know his voice." (John 10:1-4)

I saw the gentle shepherd yesterday. He didn't have a beard. He was much younger than one might expect; he is our cherished Grade 8 teacher. He had a flock that could scatter at any given moment. It was obvious to me that a number of the sheep in his flock had been frightened by past experiences with the "wolf," who is really a personification of their inner compulsions, fears and obsessions. This can make them skittish, easily scattered and readily misled. I watched in admiration as this young shepherd cared for his flock and commanded them with gentleness and firmness. In Christ's proverbial flock, there were 100 sheep, of which only one fled. In this shepherd's flock, there were upwards of ten sheep that might bolt at any given minute. Yet, this flock knew the voice of its shepherd; he quietly reminded them that when they heard his voice, it was time to come back as a flock again. Never was their dignity compromised by the call of the shepherd, in spite of their constant butting against the figurative fences that were erected for their own good.

It was Jesus who taught us that the good shepherd lays down his life for his sheep. Our good shepherd has the courage to lay down his life in the form of a vocation to the seemingly endless flocks that pass through the gate of his classroom. He is the pastor of the pasture, providing for their physical, intellectual, social, psychological and spiritual welfare. I have personally witnessed him pining to become more involved with one of his most troubled lambs, as he sought out the experts to ask what else he could do to help this child. It was truly fitting that we were literally walking on green pastures yesterday (at our confirmation retreat), complete with valleys and shadows, yet this flock feared not as they played under the watchful eye of the good shepherd.

## ENCULTURATING CATHOLIC CHARACTER

### Experience

Who, in your life experience, is a good shepherd?

### Understanding

In what ways is the particular virtue of courage related to the qualities of the good shepherd?

### Reflection

(P) In what ways has your own courage played a role in your spiritual development?

(C) Which voice does our community respond to? Which gate does it lead us through?

### Reorientation

(P) Who, in your care, do you need to shepherd? Through which gate will you lead them?

(C) What is one action that our school can take toward building a collective commitment to good shepherding?

# II. JUSTICE

*Please follow the methodology outlined under the particular virtue of faith (or see the section entitled Methodology at the end of the book).*

What is this notion of justice? Certainly we have a common-sense notion of justice, where it is seen as a consequence for one's actions, and needs to be proportionate to the crime committed. But there is another notion of justice, one that has a transcendent dimension to it, lifting it from our earthly conceptions to one that is conditioned by the unconditional (the love of Jesus). Jesus died for the sins of others. What sort of justice was that? In this kind of justice, there was no sense of retribution, only resurrection to a higher form of being. The following stories are intended to connect our life experiences to a transcendent notion of justice.

# 17. THE AXIS MUNDI

Joshua spoke to the Lord; and he said in the sight of Israel:

**"Sun, stand still at Gibeon,**
**and Moon, in the valley of Aijalon."**
**And the sun stood still, and the moon stopped ….**
**(Joshua 10:12-13)**

The axis mundi is a cross-cultural symbol representing the point of intersection between heaven and earth. At this point, in cultural mythology, communication occurs between the two. In so many ways, our school is the axis mundi for the lives of a number of our students. It is the place where communication occurs from the depths of our vulnerable students' being (they may be wounded, misunderstood, disoriented) to the comparatively higher realm of our being (when we witness compassion, understanding, orientation). Some say that the axis mundi is the still point of the cosmos, where eternity exists and around which the universe revolves. Others have suggested that the cross of crucifixion represents the axis mundi, where the four compass directions (as represented by the cross itself) merged with heaven and earth at the moment of Christ's death, representing the universality of Christ's salvific mission. I think that for each of you there are a number of students for whom you are the axis mundi, the still point where woundedness and healing, doubt and compassion, uncertainty and understanding, disorientation and love, injustice and justice meet in a moment of nascent redemption. In such moments, you model the promise of the Kingdom and allow not only our students' souls, but your own, to re-enact in a very human way the blessing that Christ brought upon the world at the moment of his death. May you glimpse the eternal this year, if only for a moment.

## ENCULTURATING CATHOLIC CHARACTER

### Experience

Recount a time when you felt that you had found a spiritual still point.

### Understanding

What was it about this experience that made it feel like a still point?

### Reflection

(P) In what way is your still point mediated by the peace of Christ?

(C) Where is our communal place of stillness for students caught in the "iron cage" of injustice?

### Reorientation

(P) In what ways do you mediate between the justice that Christ witnessed and the injustice of our vulnerable children's circumstance?

(C) How can we build a communal capacity to mediate between the peace of Christ and the injustice of our vulnerable children's circumstance?

# 18. THE PERFECT CLASS

As he walked by the Sea of Galilee, he saw two brothers, Simon, who is called Peter, and Andrew his brother, casting a net into the lake—for they were fishermen. And he said to them, "Follow me, and I will make you fish for people." Immediately they left their nets and followed him. As he went from there, he saw two other brothers, James son of Zebedee and his brother John, in the boat with their father Zebedee, mending their nets, and he called them. Immediately they left the boat and their father, and followed him.... As Jesus was walking along, he saw a man called Matthew sitting at the tax booth; and he said to him, "Follow me." And he got up and followed him. (Matthew 4:18-22; 9:9)

There is no doubt that the needs of each class vary. There can seem to be a lack of justice in the distribution of demands and resources. Think about the "perfect class." Imagine a class in which none of the students suffered from the encumbrances that diminish their minds, hearts or souls. You just walk in and teach the curriculum and all the students "get it." You go home at the end of the day without the anxiety of bearing heartfelt concerns for the students who are going home to less than ideal situations or those who struggle to keep up.

Jesus could have set up his class with the ideal disciples. Instead he selected the hard to educate, the socially isolated, and even those with psycho-spiritual problems. He could have taught in the Temple to the intellectual elite, who were impressed with his knowledge of scripture. But he chose to teach those who were largely devalued by the ruling authorities of the time. His teachings transformed their lives. He took a group of people who felt they were of little value and taught them that, in the eyes of God, they were loved and precious. Most of these people would never be the same.

The students of the perfect class have many supports; the teacher, while important, need not be the agent of transformation. In the eyes of God, we are called to seek the good and to do justice in our school in spite of inadequate resources (a societal problem). Our children are his children and he has blessed us with a challenge as well: that of tipping the scales of justice in favour of those who are the most marginalized. "Blessed are those who hunger and thirst for righteousness [justice], for they will be filled" (Matthew 5:6).

## ENCULTURATING CATHOLIC CHARACTER

### Experience

Recount an instance when you witnessed someone undergoing a personal transformation (not necessarily an immediate one or a dramatic one).

### Understanding

What role did a sense of personal growth play in this transformation?

### Reflection

(P) What feelings does the concept of justice engender in you? In which direction do those feelings orient you (toward the commonsense idea or the notion of the transcendent)?

(C) What is one area of our school that suffers from a lack of justice?

### Reorientation

(P) What is one area in your life in which the notion of justice is being undermined? How can you seek the good in this situation?

(C) What commitment do we need to make to ensure that our communal ethos is one of resurrection?

# 19. THE "MULTICOLOURED TUNIC"

**Now Israel loved Joseph more than any other of his children, because he was the son of his old age; and he had made him a long robe with sleeves [multicoloured tunic]. (Genesis 37:3)**

Sometimes things occur during the course of the week that seem so unjust. The unexpected transfer of a student this past week caught me by surprise and perturbed a deep layer of ferment within me. While some might expect my response to be one of relief and even elation at the transfer of this child, I felt none of that. Instead, I felt like a cloud of disquiet had enveloped my sensibilities. How could this be? Don't the parents know how much we've cared for this child? Don't they know the resources we've painstakingly begged, borrowed and, dare I say, stolen, for this child? Just when we had started to see the faintest glimmer of hope illuminate his fledging persona, he is taken from us. It seemed so unjust. "God, how could you let this happen?"

God's silence can be deafening sometimes, like a mother's, when asked a question to which the answer should be known. God's response came out of the wisdom of silence: "He's not your child; he's mine. Your school has done its work and I'm thankful for that. Your efforts fashioned his tunic of becoming, but the tunic is his and in his moment of glorification, he will return to me in his 'multicoloured tunic.' On that day, all the sinews of your labour and that of the others I have entrusted him to, which have robed him in his earthly journey, will be torn apart to reveal the person I have always loved."

## ENCULTURATING CATHOLIC CHARACTER

### Experience

Share a time when you felt that you were simply stitching a child back together.

### Understanding

What role did your thread play in the formation of a "multicoloured tunic" for this child?

### Reflection

(P) The love of Israel for Joseph can be seen as being preferential. Which children, in your care, engender feelings of preferential treatment? How are these feelings linked to your notion of justice?

(C) Which group of children in our care is in need of preferential treatment? Why?

### Reorientation

(P) What type of thread do you sew into your students' lives?

(C) In what ways can we, as a school community, rededicate ourselves to building an ethos of "tailored justice" (one that responds to specific needs)?

# 20. YOU SHALL SHINE LIKE THE STARS IN HEAVEN

**Those who are wise shall shine like the brightness of the sky, and those who lead many to righteousness [justice], like the stars forever and ever. (Daniel 12:3)**

The part of the sky that Daniel refers to was considered to be the eighth sphere, which contained our solar system, with the earth at its centre. Staff in a school occupy a very lofty ethereal space in the eighth sphere of the universe, as they are often identified with the wise (those who work for justice). What greater reward could there be than to have the promise of shining like the "stars forever"? There are many roads that we tread on our journey toward justice. It is apparent to me that a school community is gifted in so many diverse ways. No single gift is to be treasured more than the others. To some is given the gift of counsel, to others right judgment, to others patience, to others wisdom, to others compassion. I have seen the impact each member of a school staff has on certain children in the community. None of us has a monopoly on giftedness; when we work collectively for the good of children, we meet the varied needs of an astonishing number of children. In doing so, we create a more just community. It is as if each of us is a different star in the sky, each with its own distinct spectrum. Yet an isolated star, no matter how bright, pales in comparison to the luminosity of the constellation of stars that form the brightness of our vocation. So let us celebrate our giftedness, our differences and our common vocation, knowing that we have been called together at this given time by God to build the Kingdom, right here at our school.

## ENCULTURATING CATHOLIC CHARACTER

### Experience

Who, in your experience, shines like a star in heaven?

### Understanding

Why would Daniel have likened a star to the wise (those who work for justice)?

### Reflection

(P) Which notion of justice is constellated by the values that guide your life: retribution or resurrection?

(C) Which notion of justice is constellated by the values that guide our school: retribution or resurrection?

### Reorientation

(P) What wisdom do you impart to your school community? How do you do it?

(C) How can we, as a school community, use our collective gifts to brighten the horizon of our school?

# III. PRUDENCE

*Please follow the methodology outlined under the particular virtue of faith (or see the section entitled Methodology at the end of the book).*

I believe that the virtue of prudence has both an intellectual and moral dimension. Intellectually, it falls under the level of conscious thought that we associate with wisdom. However, in its moral dimension, it refers to the level of consciousness that is concerned with the pursuit of good through doing the right thing. It is not enough to know the right thing to do; we must also commit to doing what is right. Often we phrase this as "the most loving thing to do" or say, "What would Jesus do?" The following stories reflect ways that staff do the right thing.

# 21. THE SPIRIT CHIME

**"Let us choose what is right; let us determine among ourselves what is good." (Job 34:4)**

I happened to be party to a conversation last week where some young ladies (not at the school) were talking about the size of someone's engagement diamond. I couldn't help but reflect on this and wonder if marriage wasn't more about the size of the promise than the size of the ring. We – as teachers, educational assistants, secretaries, custodians, child and youth workers or principal – recognize the promise in our students, but I wonder how often we recognize the promise in ourselves. As humans, we are self-constituting beings, which means that we become what we know, value and do. As people who live out their lives in schools, we have the sacred opportunity of fulfilling our own personal promise through our vocations, as was the case for one teacher this week. One of our students was having a particularly bad day. He was tormenting a number of other students, not to mention his teacher. Our cherished itinerant teacher, moved by the compassion in his heart, gave of his time to teach this little child how to spin a hula hoop and then helped him piece together a wind chime. He was trying to help the young lad piece together the chime of his own broken spirit. Their conversation was gently permeated with this sage's counsel on doing the right thing in times of turmoil. He was the fatherly figure that this child had been denied. It was as if the inharmonic tones in the life of the child were being harmonized by the spiritual overtone of the teacher. The Hebrew word for wind and spirit come from the same root, *ruach*, meaning that this was more than a wind chime - it was a spirit chime, one that sounds the fulfillment of the promise of both teacher and student.

## ENCULTURATING CATHOLIC CHARACTER

### Experience

Recount a time when you had the experience of an invisible force.

### Understanding

In what ways is the metaphor of the wind an appropriate symbol for the dynamism of the spirit?

### Reflection

(P) What image would you use to represent your own spirituality? Explain.

(C) Which melody would you identify as the collective spiritual chime of our school?

### Reorientation

(P) In what ways does the invisible spirit drive you to do the right thing for the students at your school? In doing so, how do you fulfill your promise as an educator?

(C) How does our collective spirit help us to fulfill the promise (doing the right thing) that we make to the children in our care?

# 22. "WHY DON'T YOU EVER TAKE ME?"

**On the other hand, those who prophesy speak to other people for their building up and encouragement and consolation. (1 Corinthians 14:3)**

A curious thing occurred in our Grade 2 class this week. Our own prophet of prudence (our child and youth worker) was taking one of her truculent little angels (who suffers from a deep-seated sense of anger as a result of traumatic experiences) from class for his weekly tune-up (otherwise known as harp lessons). As she was leaving the class, one of our quieter students asked, "Why don't you ever take me?" Our CYW, who is not often at a loss for words, fumbled to merge the innocence of the question with the politics of the answer. If only we had the resources to totally eliminate the need for political responses! A society that valued the marginalized would ensure that there was enough funding to serve all pupils in need. That is not our reality, despite the best of intentions, and while we are called to advocate on behalf of all students in special need, we are also called to be prudent in our response to the reality we face. Wisdom recognizes that the answers are not easy, but the questions must be raised. What is the most loving thing to do? What is the right thing to do? What would Jesus do? Certainly our prophet the CYW has done much to build up, encourage and console the special children in her care.

## ENCULTURATING CATHOLIC CHARACTER

### Experience

Recount a story where someone's prudence (knowing the right thing to do) revealed a wisdom that was beyond the grasp of common sense.

### Understanding

What was it about that revealed wisdom that transcended common knowledge?

### Reflection

(P) What are your most prudent inclinations? Are they infused with a wisdom that goes beyond the grasp of common sense?

(C) What is one prudent action that we, as a community, collectively take to building up, encouraging or consoling the children in our care?

### Reorientation

(P) What do you need to do to make sure that your sense of prudence is based in wisdom?

(C) How can we, as a school community, enlighten our codes of prudence (codes of conduct) with a commitment to building up, encouraging and consoling?

# 23. "YOU HAVE HIDDEN THESE THINGS"

"But to what will I compare this generation? It is like children sitting in the marketplaces and calling to one another, 'We played the flute for you, and you did not dance; we wailed, and you did not mourn.'" ... At that time Jesus said, "I thank you, Father, Lord of heaven and earth, because you have hidden these things from the wise and the intelligent and have revealed them to infants; yes, Father, for such was your gracious will." (Matthew 11:16-18, 25-30)

It was another of many case conferences we have for our children, with several representatives from community agencies as well as our special education resource teachers, teachers, educational assistants and child and youth worker in attendance. Once again we were being asked to take into account the specific cognitive, emotional, behavioural, psychological and social needs of a child. It can seem overwhelming at times: structuring a class with multiple groups at different levels in reading and writing, putting in place several different plans for students with IEPs, and then a new student arrives. There is something sacred about our school in that we seem to have been chosen to be the refuge of so many of the lost sheep of the Kingdom. (Perhaps every school feels this way!) When others look upon our school, they don't see what we see, because God has "hidden these things from the wise and intelligent and revealed them to infants" (Matthew 11:25). Here Jesus is referring to those who have undergone the birth of a new heart of consciousness. And so, each and every day, at whatever station we have in this sacred place, we stand at the door saying, "Come to me, all you that are weary and are carrying burdens, and I will give you rest ... for I am gentle and humble of heart, and you will find rest for your souls" (Matthew 11:29-30).

At the end of our meeting, the woman from a local community agency (who had seen many jurisdictions in her storied career) paused to say thank you to our school for its willingness to help children.

## ENCULTURATING CATHOLIC CHARACTER

### Experience

Recount a story of a child where something that was hidden suddenly burst forth to proclaim itself.

### Understanding

What was it about that something that caused the child to hide it?

### Reflection

(P) Is there something that speaks from your immediate (childlike) experience of God that has remained hidden in your heart? What is it?

(C) Is it possible for a community to have an immediate (prior to objectification in words) experience of God? If so, what was experienced?

### Reorientation

(P) Do you think that consciousness of both the immediate and mediated (religion) experiences of God are needed in order to be prudent?

(C) How can we discern the hidden voice of our collective calling amid the voices of a culture that communicates a different message?

# 24. THE PRUDENT TEACHER

"I, wisdom, live with prudence,
and I attain knowledge and discretion." (Providence 8:12)

"I want to compliment you," said the veteran educational psychologist as she peered above the rim of her reading glasses, a rim that was often her estimation of a teacher's worth. She had been in many conferences with teachers, and even though she had the utmost respect for good teachers, the deeply etched furrow in her brow betrayed her dismay on other occasions, where her prescription for success had fallen upon deaf ears. In such cases, her eyes remained fixed below the rim and her intentions on the facts of the report. She raised her eyes above the rim to focus on our Grade 6 teacher, whose quick wit often deflected praise because his inner constitution demanded his own perfection. He was now slumped in a seizure of humility. "It's not often that we see such high regard for teachers on these reports," she continued, "but your student indicated that she respected you because your class was strict and yet fun, and that's exactly what this child needs." I sat at the meeting doubly proud of my new teacher, as minutes before this meeting I had witnessed the heartfelt thanks of two parents who were initially reluctant to put their child on an IEP, feeling it was an excuse to accept failure. They now saw the rewards of such a step. There's no such thing as failure in this teacher's class: his climate of high expectations and strict rules was infused with a love for children. Today, however, the impossible standards he held for himself were tempered by the affectionate praise of his student, one who might otherwise have been a lost lamb in the field of education.

## ENCULTURATING CATHOLIC CHARACTER

### Experience

Recount an occasion where you felt humbled by the praise of a student.

### Understanding

What role did wisdom play in the story?

### Reflection

(P) What is most praiseworthy about you?

(C) What are the praises that are sung by the students about our school?

### Reorientation

(P) How can you use a "spirituality of praise" to affect the children in your care?

(C) How can we build a culture of prudent praise (praising the wisdom behind the prudent action) in our school?

# IV. TEMPERANCE

*Please follow the methodology outlined under the particular virtue of faith (or see the section entitled Methodology at the end of this book).*

To my mind, the virtue of temperance serves as a pathway to the good. I'm not referring to the particular goods that lead to the satisfaction of the basic drives of life: hunger, thirst, pleasure, and so on. I'm referring to the notion of good that is achieved through the pursuit of value. We often mix up our spiritual drive with the instinctual drive for satisfaction, which can lead to living lives based solely on the avoidance of pain and the pursuit of pleasure. It reminds me of occasions when the wires of our neural impulses get crossed; we think we are hungry when we are really thirsty, and choose compulsive eating to satiate our misdirected need for water. To walk the path of temperance is to negotiate a path of humility, as someone does who is in touch with the simple but value-laden trajectory of a life lived with a sense of meaning and purpose. It is a path that avoids the extremes of zealous passion and futile impotence. The path begins by living in harmony with Christ, the prince of peace. It is a profoundly spiritual journey to ever-higher levels of consciousness. Blessed are the temperate: for theirs is the Kingdom of heaven. The following stories illustrate the importance of the dispositions of humility and harmony in discerning the pathway of temperance.

# 25. THE HUMBLERS

**"He has told you, O mortal, what is good; and what does the Lord require of you but to do justice, and to love kindness, and to walk humbly with your God?" (Micah 6:8)**

Something funny happened to me this week; if you don't believe me, ask our beloved Grade 3 teacher, for she was a witness. We were out on yard duty when one of our Grade 2 girls said, "Look, I've got hair like Mr. Laxton's." We both looked at her with a little confusion: what was it about her young flowing locks that could possibly resemble the thinning, well-weathered hair of Mr. Laxton? We both missed what was obvious to this little one: covered in snow, she retorted, "My hair is all white, just like his!" Of course it took our dear Grade 3 teacher a good five minutes to stop laughing, and then only because she had to point out that her locks were more like the young girl's than mine.

Children gift us with the perspective of humility, as their assessment of our various attributes are unguarded and boast an honesty that is difficult to rebuff. In reflecting on this occurrence, I've come to see that temperance, when understood as walking the path of humility, means taking the middle road between overstated and understated self-appreciation. Somewhere in the middle, we find the self in its tunic of humility. Blessed are the humble – and in this case, the humblers as well.

## ENCULTURATING CATHOLIC CHARACTER

### Experience

Recount a time when you were humbled by the honest but innocent appraisal of another person.

### Understanding

What was the "good" in that humbling experience?

### Reflection

(P) What areas of your life suffer from intemperance (excessive, compulsive) and would benefit from a reordering of priorities in alignment with what you value as being meaningful?

(C) Do we have a culture of temperance in our school? Do we walk humbly with the Lord?

### Reorientation

(P) Toward what destination does your path lead the children in your care?

(C) How can we build upon our commitment to the virtue of temperance? What would be a good first step in the building of a more temperate ethos?

# 26. THE GIFT

[T]he fruit of the Spirit is love, joy, peace, patience, kindness, generosity, faithfulness, gentleness, and self-control. There is no law against such things. And those who belong to Christ Jesus have crucified the flesh with its passions and desires. If we live by the Spirit, let us also be guided by the Spirit. (Galatians 5:22-25)

There are some stories that need to be told. This is one of those stories. Christmas is an occasion of great excitement as children wait to see what Santa has brought them. Children also have generous intents, as witnessed by their giving gifts to their teachers. I find their motives honest and sincere, but for most students, there is no cost in gift-giving. Mom (sometimes Dad) buys the gift for the teacher; the child may wrap it and deliver it. For some children, though, Mom and Dad struggle to make ends meet. This story is about one of those children.

His Grade 4 teacher was quite surprised when, on the last day before Christmas break, she was presented with a gift from this needy child, who had many more challenges than the other children in the class. You can imagine the thoughts that went through the teacher's head. The box was wrapped with more care than style. When the teacher lifted the lid, there, hidden amid some newspaper, was the little boy's favourite toy. It was a well-manipulated "transformer." It was as if the child recognized that this teacher had been the transformer in his life and he was symbolically expressing his appreciation. This was truly a gift of the fruit of his spirit. If the virtue of temperance is witnessed in humility and if humility is an accurate assessment of one's state of being, then this little boy's undervalued sense of self would have left him below the threshold of the humble. If the whole story be known, the teacher had, through her care and concern, given this young boy the gift of herself to love. It was out of this enlarged sense of self that he gave of himself back in the gift to the teacher. Blessed are the humble, for they will transform the earth.

## ENCULTURATING CATHOLIC CHARACTER

### Experience

Recount a time when someone gave a gift out of their poverty.

### Understanding

In what sense is the way someone receives a gift an indication of their temperance?

### Reflection

(P) In what way is your giftedness "guided by the Spirit"?

(C) In what way is our school oriented toward the reception of giftedness?

### Reorientation

(P) Which gift do you possess that you give freely to the children in your care?

(C) In what way can we build up our capacity to receive the giftedness of our community?

# 27. HIDDEN BLESSING

"[The temperate person] … must be hospitable, a lover of goodness, prudent, upright, devout, and self-controlled." (Titus 1:8)

I've been struggling to figure out how to engage, serve and redirect one of our troubled little souls. Alienated, for the most part, from his classmates, unable to understand or keep up in class, in spite of the heroic efforts of his teacher and other staff and volunteers, he has begun the slow process of retreat from the normal flow of the world. His frustration is often expressed in angry outbursts at the phantoms of his despair. Yet, as he is a child of God, we are asked to have eyes that penetrate the layers of armour that protect his soul and to discover that nascent flame of hope, kindled by his inherent dignity. That can be difficult at times, especially when we are charged with the responsibility of helping not only him, but also those children who may be caught in his wrath of frustration. Yet, once again, I was called to see through God's eyes as I walked down the Junior Kindergarten corridor. There I saw our tormented soul with the JKs; at first, I must admit, I was seized by suspicion and doubt as I wondered what he was up to. I felt a flush of protective fear for our littlest souls. It took only the grace of a moment's hesitation to see the real child, unfettered by the tribulations of adolescence, as he caringly zipped up jackets, patted the backs of the little ones with encouragement and escorted them out to recess. If only to confirm my observation, our own saint of the afflicted, our loving JK teacher, sought me out after school to let me know what a fantastic helper this lost soul had been. I thank God for moments like this and I also thank this very special teacher for her tiny JK corral of holiness, where I have often asked her to embrace a number of our children and to provide them with the opportunity to unleash their hidden blessing.

## ENCULTURATING CATHOLIC CHARACTER

### Experience

Who in your life has witnessed the virtue of temperance (self-control) for you?

### Understanding

How did this experience shape you?

### Reflecting

(P) In which area of your life are you most temperate? Which area requires more temperance?

(C) If we took the "grace of a moment's hesitation," what "hidden blessing" might we find in our school?

### Reorientation

(P) What can you do in your role to allow others to unleash their "hidden blessing"?

(C) How can we build into our school routines opportunities for our troubled souls to unleash their "hidden blessing"?

# 28. THE WOLF AND THE LAMB

**The wolf will live with the lamb,
the leopard will lie down with the goat,
the calf and the lion and the yearling together;
and a little child will lead them. (Isaiah 11:6)**

Sometimes you see the fruits of your labour, even if it's only a glimpse. It can happen in a way that is like the opening and closing of the diaphragm on a camera lens, which captures for long-term memory a single frame in the ever unfolding story of life. I had just made an announcement prohibiting cross-divisional play of students due to minor incidents on the playground when, much to my dismay, I saw Grade 2, 3, 4, 5, 6 and 7 students playing soccer together. As I approached the field, the younger children read my undisguised intent and quickly intercepted me, pleading their case: "Mr. Laxton, the older kids are being good to us; they're not pushing or anything!" I watched the game for the next 30 minutes and marvelled at the tact and discretion the older students were showing to the younger ones. They were, in fact, living in right relationship with one another. It reminded me of the passage from Isaiah, which announced that one of the signs of the coming of the Messiah was that the "wolf will live with the lamb." There were certainly a number of lambs with occasional wolf-like tendencies out on the field, and yet for this moment in time, goodwill was the rule of the day. I felt grateful to all those who contributed to bringing about this moment in the building of the Kingdom. Their daily witness to the good news leads to a destination of ethereal harmony. As moments like this become more frequent, the snapshots become more continuous in the life of the community and play like a feature film, no longer just a momentary glance.

## ENCULTURATING CATHOLIC CHARACTER

### Experience

Recount an instance when you witnessed an occasion of complete social harmony (social good).

### Understanding

What is it that brings you into harmony with another person or group of persons?

### Reflection

(P) When is it that you feel in harmony with God?

(C) When is that we as a community exist in social harmony?

### Reorientation

(P) In those temperate moments in your life, who is really "in control"?

(C) How can our school build a collective notion of temperance, such that it brings us into a deeper experience of harmony?

# COMMUNAL VIRTUES

*Read the definition (to yourself or as a group) of the communal virtues to provide an overall context for the particular virtue.*

The communal virtues I have selected reflect those that have a varied status within Catholic tradition. Some are considered to be subsumed under other values (for example, gratitude is subsumed by justice in the thoughts of St. Aquinas); others are associated with Catholic Character Themes (from the Eastern Ontario Catholic Curriculum Cooperative). I simply posit the following particular virtues as being important to the formation of character and community.

# I. GRATITUDE

*Begin by writing your own definition of the particular virtue in question.*

*Then read the description below (to yourself or as a group) before exploring any of the reflections under this particular virtue.*

There are many notions of gratitude. Some of the common sense ones don't resonate with the religious meaning of gratitude. In some interpretations, gratitude is expressed in terms of our indebtedness to God for creating us. I don't think God would want us to feel indebted. I believe God wants us to feel loved. In the religious sense, our very being has been created to know and feel the unrestricted love of our Creator. This is the religious experience of bliss or joy. Gratitude is a feeling that responds to the unconditional love of God. This feeling is part of the *eros* (desire) of the human spirit, lifting us upward to love God more completely. We bear the fruit of the virtue of gratitude when, out of our enlarged capacity, we love our neighbour. In the light of the aforementioned, thanksgiving can be understood as the spontaneous response of love in the heart-to-heart encounter with the other, as expressed in the commandment to "love your neighbour as yourself" (Mark 12:31).

*Now reconsider your definition of "gratitude": Is there anything you would change? If you are facilitating a group situation, allow time for participants to share their definitions in small groups. Ask the groups to come up with a definition of gratitude and then share it with the large group. Invite the groups to record their definitions for posting in a "Virtues" corner.*

# 29. THANKS "FOR ME!"

*Read the scripture quote.*

**By the grace of God I am what I am, and his grace toward me has not been in vain. (1 Corinthians 15:10)**

*Reconsider your most recent definition of the particular virtue. Is there anything you would change? Groups: Allow time for discussion and feedback to the large group. Individuals: Journal your response.*

*Read the story.*

We have much to be thankful for. I was reminded of that by two occurrences in our school this week. In our cherished Senior Kindergarten teacher's class, the students had rehearsed the words of a song of thanksgiving. When they were asked what they were thankful for, each recited the typical responses of young children. Then our devoted educational assistant was asked what she was thankful for. Before she could answer, her very special student, who rarely articulates a single word clearly, blurted out "For me!"

It reminded me of the biblical story (1 Samuel 3:1-10) where Samuel kept hearing someone call his name. Each time he checked to see if it was Eli, the priest he was serving, but it wasn't. Finally, Eli figured out that it was God speaking. Our little miracle of lucidity was surely God speaking to our devoted EA, thanking her for all she has done and, by association, thanking the rest of us for all we do. The second moment came in our beloved Grade 3 teacher's class, when I was invited to listen to the students' thank you rhymes in the form of couplets. Each couplet was crafted with care, reflecting their thankfulness for everything from dogs to frogs. It is interesting that the children's couplets and discipleship have something in common. The early Christian community sent disciples out two at a time, in couplets. They, too, used the power of the word to express their gratitude to God. I felt a bit like Jesus sitting there, with children at my feet reading me their words of thanks and our beloved teacher ever-present as the architect of this holy moment.

*Reflect on the story:*

Does the story strike a chord with your experience? If so, try to identify not only the chord, but also the underlying value. If not, does it strike a note of discord? If so, why?

- *If you are in a group situation, allow time for group feedback on a voluntary basis.*

- *If you are doing this on your own, journal your thoughts for later reflection.*

## ENCULTURATING CATHOLIC CHARACTER

### Experience

*Write your response to the statement below. If in a group, share your response with the group. Each group will select one story to share with the large group.*

Recount a time when your source of gratitude came not from indebtedness, but from joy.

### Understanding

*Write your response to the question below. If in a group, on a voluntary basis, share your response with the group. Have each group, on a voluntary basis, share one response with the large group.*

What is your understanding of the relationship between gratitude and grace ("by the grace of God I am what I am")?

## Reflection

Write your response to the personal (P) question given under "Reflection." If in a group, on a voluntary basis, share your response with the group. Groups may, on a voluntary basis, share a story with the large group. The facilitator may skip the personal question and move to the community (C) question. Each group should be given the opportunity to share their response to the community question.

(P) What role has grace played in your personal sense of gratitude?

(C) Do we have a communal sense of gratitude? What is the gratitude for?

## Reorientation

*Answer the personal (P) questions and if in a group situation, the community (C) question. The facilitator will have each group report back to the main group. The facilitator may record the responses to the community (C) question and work toward a communal discernment of a praxis to which all are willing to make a commitment.*

(P) How might the act of greeting the start of each day with the attitude of gratitude change the nature of your interactions with the children in your care?

(C) How can we build a deeper sense of gratitude into each day that we have together?

# 30. "GLAD AND GENEROUS HEARTS"

They devoted themselves to the apostles' teaching and fellowship, to the breaking of bread and the prayers. Awe came upon everyone, because many wonders and signs were being done by the apostles. All who believed were together and had all things in common; they would sell their possessions and goods and distribute the proceeds to all, as any had need. Day by day, as they spent much time together in the temple, they broke bread at home and ate their food with glad and generous hearts, praising God and having the goodwill of all the people. And day by day the Lord added to their number those who were being saved. (Acts 2:42-47)

One of our little guys told his teacher that his family didn't have much money and couldn't afford groceries. Of course the teacher was horrified at his situation and at the fact that he had expressed this in front of the entire class. As she was gasping for air, another child in the class piped up, saying, "That's okay, my family can't afford food either, but the church gives us food and I can ask them to give his family food, too." The church, in discerning the needs of its community and acting on them, allows families to restore the balance they need in their lives to live with dignity. The child, who was perfectly honest about his situation, spoke in true humility. I grew in appreciation and gratitude for the acts of the early Christian communities, where "they broke bread at home and ate their food with glad and generous hearts, praising God and having the goodwill of all the people." For the first time, I grasped the relationship between glad and generous hearts, gratitude and building community. Certainly our own little disciple who piped up after hearing his classmate's comment had a "glad and generous heart," praising God through the acts of our own contemporary Christian community.

## ENCULTURATING CATHOLIC CHARACTER

### Experience

Recount an occasion when you praised God with a "glad and generous heart."

### Understanding

How is the notion of gratitude related to having a "glad and generous heart"?

### Reflection

(P) What is your source of gladness?

(C) In what ways do we devote ourselves "to the apostles' teaching and fellowship, to the breaking of bread and the prayers"?

### Reorientation

(P) What role does having a "glad and generous heart" play in your daily vocation with children?

(C) How can we build a communal ethos of "glad and generous hearts"?

# 31. THE LORD'S TABLE

As they [disciples] came near the village to which they were going, he walked ahead as if he were going on. But they urged him strongly, saying, "Stay with us, because it is almost evening and the day is now nearly over." So he went in to stay with them. When he was at the table with them, he took bread, blessed and broke it, and gave it to them. Then their eyes were opened, and they recognized him; and he vanished from their sight. They said to each other, "Were not our hearts burning within us while he was talking to us on the road, while he was opening the scriptures to us?" (Luke 24:28-32)

Sometimes you realize that you're at the Lord's table, and you aren't in church. I had a profound sense of gratitude last week as I sat in a room full of adults around our brand new table in the special education resource teacher's room. We had all gathered to dialogue about the welfare of one of our special little children. These meetings can sometimes be a game of pass the buck, and it's usually the school that ends up with the buck, but this meeting had a different flow to it. That was thanks largely to our SERT, our educational assistant and the teacher, as well as the gentle manner of the woman from community mental health. It was obvious that our teacher and EA were way ahead of pace; they had already tried every suggestion the group had for them. In addition to that, they had suggestions for the other members of the shared services meeting to put in their back pockets. I could see that the three ladies from our staff knew the boy by heart, and if faith is knowledge born of love, then the faith of these women was an occasion of immense gratitude.

For a moment, as I looked around the table at all the women who were gathered for this one little boy (including his mother and former caregivers), I envisioned myself sitting with the disciples at the table of the Lord. Don't for a minute suppose that because I was the only male at the table that I saw myself as Jesus. Not at all. Jesus' place was present once again in the form of a broken body – this time it was the body of the little boy for whom we had all gathered. He had brought us to a table from which much good issued and much gratitude was in evidence. I am grateful for our Grade 1 teacher, EA and SERT for being present at the foot of the cross for this child every day that he is with us.

## ENCULTURATING CATHOLIC CHARACTER

### Experience

Recount a time when sharing a meal evoked a sense of gratitude.

### Understanding

What were you so thankful for?

### Reflection

(P) What role did feelings play in your sense of gratitude? How often are you animated by a spirit of gratitude?

(C) Where is the Lord's table located in our school?

### Reorientation

(P) Where is the Lord's table situated in your life? Who do you need to invite to the table?

(C) How do we go about building a table large enough for everyone? How can we gather more frequently at this table?

# 32. THE SCHOOL VILLAGE

**And let the peace of Christ rule in your hearts, to which indeed you were called in the one body. And be thankful. Let the word of Christ dwell in you richly; teach and admonish one another in all wisdom; and with gratitude in your hearts sing psalms, hymns, and spiritual songs to God. And whatever you do, in word or deed, do everything in the name of the Lord Jesus, giving thanks to God the Father through him. (Colossians 3:15-17)**

If it takes a village to raise a child, how many villages does it take to raise a school full of children? The answer is obviously a number much larger than the number of staff we have and, in truth, the whole community needs to be involved in raising the children.

There are occasions when staff, out of the generosity of their inexhaustible spirits, pitch in to help when something's gone awry, as was the case recently. I had been in my office at the end of one of those seemingly interminable Fridays, with a parent who had concerns of her own. Much time had elapsed since the end of school; I walked through my doorway to find several staff entertaining one of our very young students, whom I was surprised to see at this late hour. The bus driver had returned the child, as his mom was not at the stop and he was too young to leave on his own. Our indefatigable secretary had at long last succumbed to the vicissitudes of one of those ubiquitous bugs that populate the recesses of the office, but in her absence this heavenly host of staff stepped in to fill the void. They had already tried to reach a relative of any description, without success. Not the types to be flustered, they engaged the child in games while we tried to figure out a solution. As luck (or maybe Providence) would have it, we noticed a rather harried mother who was pushing a stroller and pulling a child in tow approach the school's front door. She literally burst through the door and burst into tears of gratitude when she saw her son. Circumstances had made it impossible for her to meet her child or call the school. My heart went out to this woman, who has much more on her plate than I could ever imagine. At the same time, my heart was filled with gratitude for the generosity of the our SK, Grade 2 and Grade 6 teachers, who put their own needs aside to minister to this young child when there was no one else available.

## ENCULTURATING CATHOLIC CHARACTER

### Experience

Recount an occasion when you witnessed your community responding to a crisis situation that went beyond the call of duty.

### Understanding

To what extent was the response driven by the personal values of the staff involved? To what degree was the aforementioned communal response driven by the collective values of the school community?

### Reflection

(P) To what extent does your heart "sing psalms" of gratitude to God?

(C) To what extent does our community "sing psalms" of gratitude to God?

### Reorientation

(P) What concrete step could you take to allow the "peace of Christ [to] rule your heart," thoughts and actions each day?

(C) Identify a collectively held value in our school community that engenders a deep sense of gratitude. How can we continue to build on this value by allowing the "peace of Christ [to] rule" in the heart of our community?

# II. COMPASSION

*Please follow the methodology outlined under the particular virtue of faith (or see the section entitled Methodology at the back of the book).*

Compassion can be a convoluted notion that is entangled with sympathy. I like to conceptualize compassion as a virtue that subsumes sympathy. Sympathy is perhaps a necessary first step, but as an end, it can sometimes stunt our personal growth from the full realization of compassion. Sympathy requires that we recognize the pain that another person is going through. Compassion, in its very etymology, speaks of a collective enterprise involving at least two people (*com*): the person who is suffering and the person who accompanies them; it also suggests that the person(s) accompanying not only understand the pain, but feel the pain (*passion*). When we practise compassion, we further our spiritual growth in the attainment of the good. We also further the growth of the one who is suffering, who grasps their inherent worth and recognizes the good that is the dynamism active both in the compassionate person's response and in themselves. This draws them ever further out of their current situation toward their full human potential. In a somewhat analogous way, Christ shares in our pain and the dynamism of his Spirit elevates us to higher states of personal holiness. The following reflections illustrate the compassionate response of staff to the needs of students in their care.

# 33. MY STAFF, THEY COMFORT ME

The Lord is my shepherd, I shall not want.
He makes me lie down in green pastures;
he leads me beside still waters;
he restores my soul.
He leads me in right paths
for his name's sake.

Even though I walk through the darkest valley,
I fear no evil;
for you are with me;
your rod and your staff
they comfort me. (Psalm 23:1-4)

The occurrences of the past week or two have cloaked my heart in heaviness; I feel as though I am walking through the psycho/social/spiritual valleys in the lives of a number of our students. They are, in many ways, held captive in their own dark valleys, as a result of being exposed to evil (biological, emotional, psychological) at the key formational periods of their lives. How lost their souls must be; how downtrodden their hearts. Their joy can be compromised by their pain, which sometimes reaches out with raptor-like precision, wounding others in order that their cries may be heard. I have walked this pathway with older children, but their defenses are so finely tuned and their coping strategies so well rehearsed that one may even be deluded into thinking they can take care of themselves. Not so for the younger vulnerable children. What is it that God asks of me at this station in my life? One thing I do know is that "(my) staff, they comfort me." I am often buoyed by the upward current of care, concern and personal sacrifice that each of them makes for the sake of our children. I have seen the misted window of their hearts as they recount the enormity of the challenges they face in their own personal station, and yet they continue to carry the cross for others, as Simon of Cyrene carried Jesus' cross for a while. I can only offer a cloth to wipe the sweat from their brow – not much compensation for the journey ahead – but in each cloth soaked by the perspiration of care, concern and compassion, I see the image of Christ's face and "I fear no evil; for you are with me."

## ENCULTURATING CATHOLIC CHARACTER

### Experience

Recount a time when you walked through the valley of darkness.

### Understanding

How was your soul restored during this journey?

### Reflection

(P) Do feelings of compassion flow freely from your heart, or are they buried in the unexamined valleys of the unconscious darkness?

(C) Do feelings of compassion flow freely from the heart of our school? When or why not?

### Reorientation

(P) How can you be a "green pasture" for the students in your care?

(C) In what ways can we, as a community, dedicate ourselves to building "green pastures" of compassion for the students in our care?

# 34. COMING ASHORE

Now when Jesus heard this, he withdrew from there in a boat to a deserted place by himself. But when the crowds heard it, they followed him on foot from the towns. When he went ashore, he saw a great crowd; and he had compassion for them and cured their sick. (Matthew 14:13-14)

I was overwhelmed with a sense of my own inadequacy as I watched one of our vulnerable children spin circles on the floor during one of our assemblies, despite the best efforts of our most empathetic educational assistant to contain his physical contortions within the realm of what is safe. I was reminded of the story in the gospel where Jesus healed those possessed by demons, and I wished that I could dispel the demon of his circumstance. A number of psychologists and theologians have speculated that some of the people Jesus cured had a psychosis, and that Jesus' caring and compassionate touch healed them of their affliction. I must admit at being a bit bewildered, within the institutional structure of the educational system and its limitations, at how to respond to this child, beyond the interventions that are in place. I do know that I feel a tremendous source of strength when I am able to walk with others on staff, as we all face these situations. Perhaps that is what Jesus meant when he said, "For where two or three are gathered in my name, I am there among them" (Matthew 18:20).

## ENCULTURATING CATHOLIC CHARACTER

### Experience

Recount a time when you felt that you had the experience of "coming ashore" (overwhelmed by the needs) in your school.

### Understanding

What role did compassion play in your "coming ashore" experience?

### Reflection

(P) How does the virtue of compassion manifest itself in your life? Is it a force in the orientation of your life?

(C) Which shore in our school do we need to "come to" with a sense of compassion?

### Reorientation

(P) How could you establish a "sacred space of compassion" in your own life?

(C) What can we, as a school community, do to build a collective consciousness of the healing power of the virtue of compassion?

# 35. TRIBUTARIES OF THE SOUL

**Then the Lord God will wipe away the tears from all faces, and the disgrace of his people he will take away from all the earth, for the Lord has spoken. (Isaiah 25:8)**

I stood there, emotionally paralyzed, watching the tears roll down the cheeks of one of our tiny children, wondering how I could remove the emotional, physical and spiritual scars of dis-grace. Children are robbed of their trust in a loving God through the violation of their innocence in the very womb of their domestic church: home. By "dis-grace" I mean a distortion in our ability to live in harmony with the grace of God. There is little doubt in my mind that the fundamental betrayal of trust in the loving ground of the universe (God) is a form of dis-grace. It occurred to me, in my tears for this child, that tears form part of the common tributary of our souls. In scripture, tears are often associated with distress and pain. Our school certainly has its sanctuary for the tearful. Not the self-pitying type of tears, but tears of anxiety and sorrow. Tears, in our culture of rugged individualism, are often shed in the recesses of our being and only rarely burst through cultural inhibitions to flow forth for all to see. As school staff, you, my people (if I may be so presumptuous and claim you as my family), are the hands that wipe away the tears of our children in need, absorbing grief by your very presence. Little do our students know that in each of you, the tears of compassion etch the landscape of your soul.

## ENCULTURATING CATHOLIC CHARACTER

### Experience

Recount an experience when something moved you to tears of compassion.

### Understanding

What was it about the experience that moved you to tears?

### Reflection

(P) Do you believe that tears of compassion etch the landscape of your soul?

(C) How do we help the children in our care who suffer from the tears of dis-grace?

### Reorientation

(P) How can you deepen the tributaries of compassion in your own soul?

(C) How can we build a community ethos dedicated to wiping away the tears of dis-grace?

# 36. THE "CHILL GRILL"

**In those days when there was again a great crowd without anything to eat, he called his disciples and said to them, "I have compassion for the crowd, because they have been with me now for three days and have nothing to eat. If I send them away hungry to their homes, they will faint on the way—and some of them have come from a great distance." His disciples replied, "How can one feed these people with bread here in the desert?" He asked them, "How many loaves do you have?" They said, "Seven." Then he ordered the crowd to sit down on the ground; and he took the seven loaves, and after giving thanks he broke them and gave them to his disciples to distribute; and they distributed them to the crowd. They had also a few small fish; and after blessing them, he ordered that these too should be distributed. They ate and were filled; and they took up the broken pieces left over, seven baskets full. (Mark 8:1-8)**

I was lucky enough to get a seat in a pretty exclusive restaurant this past week, without a reservation and at prime time. You should all try it – it's called the "Chill Grill" and you can get reservations by dialing ONE-LOVING-EA! The compassionate chef was a no-nonsense type of cook, but her huge heart was evident in the children she served. She had three special customers that day. One of them I could barely see over the horizon of the table, save for his spectacles, which, when he was at full alert, appeared as the rising sun. This sunrise was unique in that it chuckled with delight. I'll have to listen to the sunrise next time I see one; who knows, perhaps this young man was one of the Lord's prophets, reminding us that we should be filled with joy at the dawn of each new day. Another customer sat quiet and still; she reminded me of the moon. In the stillness of the moment, her charms issue forth, beckoning us to see the numinous in the luminous. The moon needs the sun to reflect its true effervescence: so, too, with this young prophetess, reminding us that we are made in God's image and that our truest reflection is that of his Son. The third client of the "Chill Grill" was an irrepressible young man who reminded me of the irrepressibility of the Holy Spirit, who takes residence in our sacred hearts. This Spirit helps us through the challenges in life by reminding us that we all have gifts. In spite of the daily challenges we face, there is a spirit about this community that is resilient, irrepressible and very sacred. When asked how many times we are to forgive, Jesus responded, "Seventy times seven" – which, in the symbolism of numbers, means infinitely. In our circumstance we are asked: How many times are we called to love? The answer is seventy times seven – which you all do.

## ENCULTURATING CATHOLIC CHARACTER

### Experience

Recount a time when you were moved to compassionate action by the hunger of another person.

### Understanding

In what ways do you think that your feeling of compassion resonates with Jesus' compassion for the hungry crowd?

### Reflection

(P) Who do you "feed" through your compassion?

(C) Who do we "feed" through our compassion?

### Reorientation

(P) Who taught you the value of compassion? How can you transform this value into a virtue?

(C) How can we build our own version of the "Chill Grill" in our community?

# III. DISCIPLESHIP

*Please follow the methodology outlined under the particular virtue of faith (or see the section entitled Methodology at the back of the book).*

To my mind, the quintessential parable on discipleship is the story of the two disciples on the road to Emmaus and the subsequent supper (Luke 24:13-32). The name "Emmaus" means "hot spring." Perhaps it symbolizes the disciples' journey to a new season of faith, one in which their "hearts were burning" with passion as scripture was opened up to them and they came to recognize Jesus during this "first Eucharist" experience. The notion of "spring" brings to mind the Easter season as well as the image of baptismal waters. Both of these images reflect the dynamism of our faith journey which, for me at least, can be engulfed in moments of confusion and searching only to be pierced by enabling instances when scripture and Eucharist coalesce in a personal awakening to the presence of Christ. The disciples in Emmaus were transformed by this experience and entered into the evangelical mission of the Church, spreading the good news of the resurrection. In our vocation as Catholic educators, we are forever journeying between Emmaus and Jerusalem, on a pilgrimage of personal conversion and evangelical mission as we prepare ourselves to educate our children.

# 37. SACRED IMPRESSIONS

**So God created humankind in his image,**
**in the image of God he created them;**
**male and female he created them. (Genesis 1:27)**

I happened to take a few minutes to drop into our Grade 1 class the other day, wanting to see them in action. They had just finished completing a booklet about the number that corresponded with their age. The students were carefully gathered on the carpet of holy imagination by their teacher, the angel of patience. It was with great pride that each student told the story of his or her existence, a narrative short in years but deeply rooted in family and tradition. It was very spiritual. Most of us spend our entire lives trying to figure out the meaning of our existence; for many of us, it can be discerned in the stories we tell. There was one little boy who has had more obstacles in his brief five years of life than I've faced in my five decades; he persisted in seeking my attention long after the others had shown me their work and were eating their snacks. He held my hand and took me around the class to point out his treasure trove of works, posted from the heights to the depths of this classroom sanctuary. I was once again struck by the sacredness of our vocation. The impact we have on children is measured in degrees of virtue, and for a number of our children, we will have impressed upon their souls our own image of God. We, as Catholics, believe that the soul forms the person; thus, ours is a vocation of sacred impressions. Perhaps, when we get to heaven, we will be surrounded by souls humbly marked with a faint vestige of our sacred impression.

## ENCULTURATING CATHOLIC CHARACTER

### Experience

What sacred image is impressed upon your soul?

### Understanding

Why do you think this image impressed itself upon your soul?

### Reflection

(P) How does this image manifest itself in your way of being in the world?

(C) What is the sacred image of our school?

### Reorientation

(P) In your call to discipleship, what are the images that you impress upon your students?

(C) How can we collectively impress our sacred image upon the souls of our students?

# 38. HEARING IS BELIEVING

**So faith comes from what is heard, and what is heard comes through the word of Christ. (Romans 10:17)**

Every once in a while I hear something that throws me back to the idealism I had when I started in this field of education. I went into teaching because I wanted to make a difference in the lives of the children I taught, and in that way contribute to making the world a better place. I must admit that I did lose my way at times, when I allowed the politics of education to blanket my ideological beliefs in a thin coat of skepticism, perhaps as a result of the constant demands I felt inadequate to meet. Fortunately, I put an untainted premium on my relationships with children; I continued to be guided by a deeply rooted calling to come out of myself and into the lives of others. Now, in the twilight years of my professional calling, I get the occasional message, via staff at our school, about former students who give me far too much credit for having had an impact on their lives. The interesting thing is that they are not thanking me for teaching them science or religion, but for teaching them to believe: in themselves, in God or in others. The other interesting thing is that the "thank you" comes from students from whom I wouldn't have expected it. I can't often remember what I said or did, but I do know that I tried to take time to inquire about how they were doing and listened when they wanted to tell me their stories. Nothing earth shattering. Perhaps that is the secret to the great lessons of life: they come from persons who do not speak as much as they listen. It is indeed gratifying to hear these anecdotes from the past. I don't relay this story to you for my self-gratification, but to encourage you to keep your idealism and not become jaded by politics or the unfairness of life. Know that you are making a difference in the lives of the children that you come into contact with, even though you may not hear about it until the next life.

## ENCULTURATING CATHOLIC CHARACTER

### Experience

Recount an occasion when you really felt that you were heard by another person.

### Understanding

What was it about the experience that let you know that you were really heard? How did that experience affect your growth as a person?

### Reflection

(P) Do you make time to listen to yourself? How do you do that? What do you hear yourself saying?

(C) What are the voices of our children calling for?

### Reorientation

(P) Which voice in your life is the one of sacredness (word of Christ)? How influential is that voice in your way of being in the world?

(C) How can we build a ministry of hearing in our school community that listens to both the call of the Spirit and the voices of children?

# 39. LIBERATED FROM THE TOMBS

As he stepped out on land, a man of the city who had de-mons met him. For a long time he had worn no clothes, and he did not live in a house but in the tombs. When he saw Jesus, he fell down before him and shouted at the top of his voice, "What have you to do with me, Jesus, Son of the Most High God? I beg you, do not torment me"— for Jesus had commanded the unclean spirit to come out of the man…Then people came out to see what had happened, and when they came to Jesus, they found the man from whom the demons had gone sitting at the feet of Jesus, clothed and in his right mind…Those who had seen it told them how the one who had been possessed by demons had been healed. (Luke 8:27-29, 35, 36)

A curious thing has been happening in our hallways, in the play-ground and in the classroom as well. One of our little guys, who has often lacked the social skills and empathy to establish meaningful friendships and as a result lacked any sort of companionship, has suddenly become the most popular guy in his class. He now comes to school with the expectation that a smile will define his face that day. This is a young lad who, until recently, rarely escaped the daily torment of a troubled spirit. You can now see him walking through the halls with a group of willing companions following him. In Luke's gospel, we read of Jesus healing a man living "in the tombs." In some-what the same way, there is a purification of this young boy's spirit happening through the healing ministry of his benevolent Grade 5 teacher and tenderhearted educational assistant. At times, he is persecuted for his odd behaviour, but through teachable moments and visions of what could be, these two disciples have facilitated an exorcism of sorts. It hasn't been an instantaneous one and is a matter of degree, but nonetheless the uneasiness of his spirit is abating. In the same gospel, Jesus spoke about the precondition to discipleship being a spirit of self-denial, a willingness to take up the cross and the desire to follow him (Luke 9:23). There is no doubt that many of you have denied yourselves and carried the burdens of your students in order to help unshackle a number of troubled souls from a life in the tombs. In doing so, you lead them to liberation in Jesus the Christ.

## ENCULTURATING CATHOLIC CHARACTER

### Experience

Recount an occasion when you witnessed someone liberated from "life in the tombs."

### Understanding

What is the difference between self-denial and life-denial (life in a tomb)?

### Reflection

(P) What role does sacred self-denial (denial of the distractions that separate us from the development of our souls) play in the formation of your own character? Why?

(C) How do we witness a culture of sacred self-denial?

### Reorientation

(P) What is one commitment that you are willing to make to a special child in your care in order to liberate them from their personal tomb?

(C) How can we, as a community, build a culture of sacred self-denial?

# 40. THE DISCIPLE'S MANDALA

**The angel of the Lord called to Abraham a second time from heaven, and said, "By myself I have sworn, says the Lord: Because you have done this, and have not withheld your son, your only son, I will indeed bless you, and I will make your offspring as numerous as the stars of heaven and as the sand that is on the seashore. And your offspring shall possess the gate of their enemies, and by your offspring shall all the nations of the earth gain blessing for themselves, because you have obeyed my voice." (Genesis 22:15-18)**

There are different models of discipleship: the apostles who were the pillars of the church; the hierarchical types of the ecclesial church; the saints and martyrs; and finally, ours, the poor shepherds who tend the sheep of the Lord in the pastures of the lay apostolate. This type of discipleship is similar to the building of a Tibetan Buddhist sand mandala. The monks form a patterned image using coloured granules of sand and then destroy it to remind themselves of the finitude of life. For each of you, the students you interact with are like the grains of sand in the emerging pattern of your own mandala. Deities are supposed to reside in the pattern of the mandala; in our case, it is Christ who resides in the pattern of our sacred encounters with students. When we take the time to reflect on the meaning of the emerging pattern of our life of vocation, as formed by the students we have affected, then we will surely find the image of Christ.

The mandala is also a symbol of wisdom and compassion that, in our circumstance, can represent our conscious intention to lead children to personal transformation. The Tibetan mandala is formed on sacred ground; so, too, is our vocation formed on the sacred ground of becoming. It reminds me of the passage in scripture where Moses approaches the burning bush, and God says, "Come no closer! Remove the sandals from your feet, for the place on which you are standing is holy ground" (Exodus 3:4-5). We slowly form the pattern of our discipleship through a lifelong vocation of discovering the holy in the ordinary sands of time. In the hourglass of life, all the subtle

116

differences we make, whether that is teaching a child to read a single letter of the alphabet or reading the lines of a child's traumatic life story, become the narrative in our mandala. Your blessings will be as numerous as "the sand that is on the seashore" and the mandala of your discipleship will survive into eternity.

## ENCULTURATING CATHOLIC CHARACTER

### Experience

Recount the story of a person whose mandala was inspiring to you.

### Understanding

What was it in their life story that spoke to you of discipleship?

### Reflection

(P) What is the image on your own mandala?

(C) What sacred image do we want to emerge on the mandala of our collective discipleship? (E.g., if the group selects Jesus, which of the four gospel images of Jesus do we want to invoke?)

### Reorientation

(P) What subtle differences would you like to make in the lives of your students?

(C) How do we go about building a culture of discipleship dedicated to the sacred image we reverence in our collective mandala?

# IV. REVERENCE

*Please follow the methodology outlined under the particular virtue of faith (or see the section entitled Methodology at the end of the book).*

Sadly, the virtue most scorned and depreciated in our knowledge-based culture is that of reverence. In no way do I intend to impugn the value of knowledge – after all, that is what we have dedicated our lives to. What I wish to suggest is that knowledge comes in many different forms. Our society places an exclusively high premium on knowledge that comes from scientific methodology. However, an arrogant culture of scientism holds that science is the sole arbiter of truth, which engenders a social attitude of irreverence for all that is sacred. Fundamentally, reverence is a virtue that is rooted in cosmology – our story of creation. Ultimately, what is at stake is the inherent meaning of our lives. Those who believe that the universe owes its origin to a benevolent Creator envision all knowledge of the good of creation as a revelation of a transcendent source of truth. As human beings, we occupy a very privileged niche in the universe, from which we not only gaze in wonder and awe at the universe "without," but also at the universe "within." Ultimately, the virtue of reverence is one that recognizes not only the transcendent source of value, but also the immanent presence of value. To hold creation in reverence is to hold oneself in reverence.

# 41. MENDING DAMAGED WINGS

**And the Word became flesh and lived among us, and we have seen his glory, the glory as of a father's only son, full of grace and truth. (John 1:14)**

Not all of God's angels get off to a good start. Some of them damage their wings on the way down, others have their wings stepped on once they get here, and some give their feathers away because they've lost the desire to fly. Our special angel (who suffers from anxiety, depression and rejection) may have experienced a combination of all of the above, but I have recently noticed that he has begun to fly again. I watched him read a story the other day, assisted by his angel of advocacy (our ever-efficacious educational assistant). While he confidently ventured into a forest of new terminology, he didn't worry about getting lost because she had given him a map: one that helped him not only decode the meaning of the words in front of him, but also the contours of his own life. If you could only have seen his face as it contorted in response to the unexpected twists and turns in the story. He smiled in sheer delight at the antics of the protagonist, who had a penchant for making bad choices and yet remained redeemably lovable. I'm sure he identified with the character in the story and probably came to realize that we human beings are of so much innate worth that we can soar beyond the bad choices we have made. I thank all who have contributed to helping this fallen angel soar on the wings of "grace and truth."

## ENCULTURATING CATHOLIC CHARACTER

### Experience

Share a personal story that had a message of deep reverence.

### Understanding

How is the notion of innate worth linked to a sense of deep reverence?

### Reflection

(P) What feelings are aroused in you in response to the notion of reverence? In which direction do they take you (e.g., an inner journey [insight] or an outer journey [actions])?

(C) What is it that is held in deep reverence by our school community?

### Reorientation

(P) How do you cultivate a sense of deep reverence for the fallen angels in your care?

(C) How can we build up a culture of reverence for our fallen angels?

# 42. IN THE BEGINNING, ORDER WAS CREATED

**In the beginning when God created the heavens and the earth, the earth was a formless void and darkness covered the face of the deep, while a wind from God swept over the face of the waters. Then God said, "Let there be light"; and there was light. And God saw that the light was good. (Genesis 1:1-4)**

What's in a bucket? I had a laugh this week when I received the provincial standardized testing booklets from one of our beloved teachers in three "buckets," as she would call them, or in three besmirched trays, as I would refer to them. Don't let the outer appearance of the vessels fool you: it is what's inside that counts. I'm referring to the collective works of our industrious Grade 3s who do their best, not in an effort to brighten the pages of the local newspaper, but in a display of their early commitment to developing an understanding of the world in order to contribute to it in meaningful ways. The appearance of the trays, however, did surprise me a little at first, as in this teacher's cosmos, the world is in perfect order. Her classroom reflects the first creation story, where God orders the watery chaos of the cosmos so that goodness may be its issue. Much good issues from this little corner of the universe. I was also reminded of the story of the Samaritan woman, who misunderstood who Jesus was. In response to Jesus' request for water, she said, "Sir, you have no bucket, and the well is deep" (John 4:11). She didn't understand that Jesus was the vessel (bucket) of the eternal waters of salvation. A number of our little ones are marked by the encumbrances of their lives, and yet we can quench their thirst from the "buckets" of our own goodness, whose source is the waters of salvation. Thanks to all whose buckets overflow with the waters of your baptismal promise.

## ENCULTURATING CATHOLIC CHARACTER

### Experience

Share a story of a time when a new sense of order quelled the waters of chaos in your life or someone else's life.

### Understanding

In what ways was a sense of spirituality implicit in the ordering that occurred in your story?

### Reflection

(P) To what extent does your sense of reverence structure your spiritual life?

(C) Which waters in our school need a "spirituality of order"?

### Reorientation

(P) How do you witness a sense of reverence for others?

(C) What can we do in our school to build a spiritual sense of order over the chaotic waters of our students' lives?

# 43. "THE NEW GIRL'S ON FIRE!"

O Lord, our Sovereign,
how majestic is your name in all the earth!

You have set your glory above the heavens.
Out of the mouths of babes and infants
you have founded a bulwark because of your foes,
to silence the enemy and the avenger.

When I look at your heavens, the work of your fingers,
the moon and the stars that you have established;
what are human beings that you are mindful of them,
mortals that you care for them? (Psalm 8:1-4)

"Out of the mouths of babes," I believe the expression goes. One of our special children was thoroughly astounded by the new girl in his class. He had, of course, noticed the new girl and was probably quite pleased that she was sitting behind him. He probably had some empathy for her, as she was new to the class and he knew how he felt in such a situation. In his mind, she was just trying to survive the first day without drawing attention to herself. As class progressed, the teacher paused to ask a question. Our special soul is someone who can appreciate what it is like to sit in class and have no idea what the answer to a question is, no matter how carefully crafted the question may be. He likely didn't notice the hand that was waving confidently behind him; he wouldn't have even expected the new girl to try to answer any questions that day. However, he quickly recognized the situation when the teacher asked the person behind him to answer the question. In quick order, the new girl gave an answer that was quite correct. Muttering his amazement to himself and in a whisper that only his educational assistant could hear, he said, "Wow, the first day, the first question and she got it right. The new girl's on fire!" There's innocence and honesty in his musing that speaks of the virtue of reverence. Our small cherub had not a morsel of resentment in his regard for the new girl, whose answer had already eclipsed his efforts and knowledge; instead, he stood in reverence of this person and her abilities. I am constantly amazed by all who work in this school. You know the meaning of injury and inequity, as you work with our special children. While we all work to bring about reverence for the human condition, not one of you has abandoned a single child in the depths of their suffering. You lighten the weight of injury and inequity by carrying their crosses for them, and in doing so you answer the psalmist's question: "What are human beings … that you care for them?"

## ENCULTURATING CATHOLIC CHARACTER

### Experience

Share a story of an occasion when something came "out of the mouths of babes" and opened your eyes to the presence of God.

### Understanding

What is it about childhood that opens us up to reverencing the human condition?

### Reflection

(P) What part of Psalm 8 speaks to your own experience of reverence? If nothing speaks to you from the Psalm, what speaks to you from your own experiences?

(C) How do we reverence our children in a way that answers the question "What are human beings … that you care for them?"

### Reorientation

(P) What does your own inner spiritual voice (in the sense of the pure experience of joy) say to you about reverencing the human condition?

(C) In what ways can our school community build a culture of reverence dedicated to deciphering the voice of "babes" amid the institutional noise?

# 44. CLEANLINESS IS A SIGN OF REVERENCE

> I will sprinkle clean water upon you, and you shall be clean from all your uncleanness, and from all your idols I will cleanse you. A new heart I will give you, and a new spirit I will put within you; and I will remove from your body the heart of stone and give you a heart of flesh.
> (Ezekiel 36:25, 26)

Long before the sun comes up, before the ice melts, before the heat is turned up, before the steps are swept, there is a presence in our school. A solitary car sits in the parking lot with the telltale fingers of Jack Frost etched on the windshield. Mother Nature can be an impertinent woman, frolicking under the cover of darkness, laying blankets of intrigue and sheets of danger. Undaunted by the frivolity of his masquerading foe, our hero faces the eternal challenge of hidden peril, stoically and relentlessly. Long after the sun has set, as the ice forms again, after the heat is turned down, after the steps have been dusted with snow, there is a presence in our school. A solitary car sits in the parking lot with the telltale fingers of Jack Frost etched on the windshield. As Mother Nature begins her nightly antics, our hero battles the relentless ebb and flow of sand, dust and grime deposited by myriad hands and feet that have been impregnated with the sheer exuberance of playing in the blankets and sheets of the bed made by Mother Nature. Undaunted by the puerility of eternal youth, our hero erases the handprints and footprints of the joy of the day that has long since faded into the night of our memories. Our dear custodians (I prefer the name "caretakers") cleanse our sacred space of all that may weaken our resolve to reach for the stars; in the process, you allow our sacred hearts to be infused with "new spirit" each and every day. Cleanliness is indeed a sign of reverence.

## ENCULTURATING CATHOLIC CHARACTER

### Experience

Recount a time when the efforts of cleansing created a sacred space in your classroom.

### Understanding

How is cleansing related to the concept of acquiring a "new heart"?

### Reflection

(P) What do you need to cleanse yourself of in order to acquire a "new spirit"?

(C) What do we as a community need to cleanse ourselves of in order to acquire a "new spirit"?

### Reorientation

(P) How would acquiring a "new heart" or a "new spirit" help you to further reverence the children in your care?

(C) How do we, as a school community, build in practices of cleansing in order to form "new hearts" in our students?

# V. SOLIDARITY

*Please follow the methodology outlined under the particular virtue of faith (or see the section entitled Methodology at the end of the book).*

I must give credit to Lech Walesa for bringing the term "solidarity" into my sphere of consciousness (my apologies to all the theologians). He was consumed with concern for the plight of the workers in Poland and organized strikes and protests on their behalf, which culminated in the formation of the Solidarity Free Trade Union. Notwithstanding much controversy, he was awarded the Nobel Peace Prize and helped move Poland from a communist state to a free democratic society. My interpretation of his mantra is that the spirit of solidarity transcends any efforts to divide and conquer. It reminds me of the biblical passage where the Roman soldiers were casting lots for Christ's clothing: "When the soldiers had crucified Jesus, they took his clothes and divided them into four parts, one for each soldier. They also took his tunic; now the tunic was seamless, woven in one piece from the top. So they said to one another, 'Let us not tear it, but cast lots for it to see who will get it.'" (John 19:23-24). It is in this reading that I discover the theological foundation of Walesa's mantra. Metaphorically speaking, the tunic represents the early Christian church, which could not be divided despite the multitude of religious, cultural, social and political forces pulling at it. St. John's community was one of solidarity that found its unification in the fabric of the Holy Spirit, one of three persons of an undivided Trinity. When we allow the Holy Spirit to guide our communal strivings, we, too, can knit a tunic of spiritual solidarity. In doing so, we permit our children to glimpse the promise of the Kingdom to come, where all will be one with the Lord.

# 45. A PRIZE-WINNING RACE

**I have fought the good fight, I have finished the race, I have kept the faith. (2 Timothy 4:7)**

It was one of those moments that made us proud to be a part of this immensely human enterprise called Catholic education. We had been competing at the local cross-country meet and many of our student athletes had put in admirable performances that day, but the moment that transcended the finitude of temporal glory occurred beyond the recognition of those who had their eyes focused on the early finishers. One of our students trailed the entire group in his race by such a margin that he was in danger of being side-swiped by many spectators who hadn't even noticed him running and had started to wander onto the course. Yet there were at least eight pairs of eyes riveted on him. One pair belonged to his effervescent teacher/coach, who sprinted across the field to offer moral support. Another pair belonged to one of the parents who is often steward to the many. The moment, however, belonged to five boys who, upon seeing him falter and about to give into the vicissitudes of his asthma, went out onto the field and flanked him in such a manner that the once inconspicuous red jersey now fused with their red jerseys to form a resplendent red banner of honour. As the boys ran past me, I heard one of the young lads, who had actually finished the same race in second place, tell our flagging star that he had the heaviest of the school jerseys and that had caused him to fall behind. I had an epiphany of sorts that day; it was of five little sacred hearts in heaven flying out past St. Peter at the "gates of Heaven" to lead a struggling soul to the eternal glory of the Lord, where all those who have finished the race win the prize.

## ENCULTURATING CATHOLIC CHARACTER

### Experience

Recount a time when you felt like you won a race even though you didn't come first.

### Understanding

What was it about finishing that race that made you feel like you had won?

### Reflection

(P) Which value(s) were implicit in the race you ran?

(C) What are the races we run as a school community?

### Reorientation

(P) Which race do you run that finishes with a strong sense of solidarity? Why?

(C) Which races do we, as a community, run that increase our commitment to solidarity? Why?

# 46. THE "SERAPHIM OF SONG"

**And suddenly there was with the angel a multitude of the heavenly host, praising God and saying, "Glory to God in the highest heaven, and on earth peace among those whom he favors!" (Luke 2:13, 14)**

A part of our Catholic tradition speaks about nine choirs of angels in heaven. It is a part of our school tradition to recognize that one of those choirs is ensconced in the ethereal timbres of our magical room of the recorder ensemble (a room whose own ninety-year-old timbers are nearly as old as the choir in heaven). The ninth choir of angels is marked with the singular ability to communicate with humankind on behalf of God. You need only search out a number of elders' homes at Christmas to see the rapture of God's tiniest messengers (our musical ensemble) as they orchestrate a musical proclamation of the coming of the Kingdom. There is solidarity of spirit in these occasions. Present, in eternal motion (arms conducting, body pulsating), is our seraphim of song, spreading cheer and musical libation to the point that elders, intoxicated by the spirit, leap to their feet and dance to the joy of days gone by. The subtle message in the music is that there is much joy to come in heaven. What better message could there be for our elders, who stand on the precipice of eternal joy themselves?

## ENCULTURATING CATHOLIC CHARACTER

### Experience

Share a story where you witnessed the special relationship that exists between students and elder members of your immediate or extended community.

### Understanding

What is it about the relationship between the young and the elders that speaks of solidarity?

### Reflection

(P) When do you experience a deep sense of solidarity?

(C) When do we, as a community, experience a deep sense of solidarity?

### Reorientation

(P) Which elders, in your own community of persons, do you have a relationship of solidarity with? What makes the relationship special?

(C) How can we, as a school community, reach out in the ways of solidarity to build an experiential ground of encounter between our young and our elders?

# 47. DELILAH'S DEMISE

> When Delilah realized that he [Samson] had told her his whole secret, she sent and called the lords of the Philistines, saying "This time come up, for he has told his whole secret to me." Then the lords of the Philistines came up to her, and brought the money in their hands. She let him fall asleep on her lap; and she called a man, and had him shave off the seven locks of his head. He began to weaken, and his strength left him. Then she said, "The Philistines are upon you, Samson!" When he awoke from his sleep, he thought, "I will go out as at other times, and shake myself free." But he did not know that the Lord had left him. (Judges 16:18-20)

Perhaps we rewrote an old biblical narrative this week at our school. According to legend, the source of Samson's strength was his hair. In his human fragility and lust for the transient beauty of life, he divulges his secret to the narrative's antagonist – Delilah. In this moment he is undone, as he becomes affixed to the pillars of vanity and finitude. This week in our school, our protagonist sloughed his hair in an act of heroism and solidarity. Unlike Samson, his strength grew that day, and the nakedness of his newly dawned scalp exposed a lack of fragility and vanity in his resolve to help others. He broke the shackles that bind children to a worldview that can be quite egocentric. I believe that his act of solidarity with children who were fighting the ravages of cancer and chemotherapy took on a holy momentum of its own. He caused our hearts to grow seven sizes that day. Our own version of Samson gazed out with wonder at a school body that chanted his name and applauded his empathy. Whether we were conscious of it or not, we were all a part of something momentous that day, something that resonates with all that is transcendent in life.

## ENCULTURATING CATHOLIC CHARACTER

### Experience

Recount a time when a seemingly small gesture of good acquired a momentum of its own, resulting in much more good being issued than was originally envisioned.

### Understanding

What was it about "the good" that galvanized people to act in solidarity?

### Reflection

(P) What is the source of good that motivates you to transcend the limits of isolation and reach out to others?

(C) How do we encourage our students to reach out in solidarity to others?

### Reorientation

(P) How can you sew seeds of solidarity in your interactions with students?

(C) How can we, as a community, build an ethos of solidarity?

# 48. "COME, YOU THAT ARE BLESSED"

"Then the king will say to those at his right hand, 'Come, you that are blessed by my Father, inherit the kingdom prepared for you from the foundation of the world; for I was hungry and you gave me food, I was thirsty and you gave me something to drink, I was a stranger and you welcomed me, I was naked and you gave me clothing, I was sick and you took care of me, I was in prison and you visited me.' Then the righteous will answer him, 'Lord, when was it that we saw you hungry and gave you food, or thirsty and gave you something to drink? And when was it that we saw you a stranger and welcomed you, or naked and gave you clothing? And when was it that we saw you sick or in prison and visited you?' And the king will answer them, 'Truly I tell you, just as you did it to one of the least of these who are members of my family, you did it to me.'" (Matthew 25:34-40)

I need to write this reflection while my heart is still embraced by the sense of euphoria that transcends the walls that limit our ability to love without fear. It's an experience similar to being in love with another human being, where we enter into a sacred space of intimacy. No, I didn't fall in love with "someone" on my recent trip to an orphanage (or Nuestros Pequenos Hermanos family, as they call themselves) in Guatemala. I fell in love with entire groups of people. I was expecting to be deeply moved by the orphans, as I had been on previous occasions. I was also expecting my heart to be warmed by the selfless devotion of the people who work and volunteer at the orphanage. I wasn't expecting to be so deeply moved by the charitable love of the group of students that we (my two very good friends, who are the original architects of these experiences, and I) took with us. What impressed me most about the students was the desire in their hearts. They were truly in search of the good. In this particular instance, they wanted to contribute to the good of social order by supporting an orphanage that depends on the generosity of its patrons. On another level, they sought to affirm the goodness of the human person by opening their hearts to a genuine human encounter of solidarity. Theirs was a mission of reconciling hardened worldviews that see the other as hostile, depraved and alien with a worldview that embraces friendship, dignity and community. These students reminded me of what the spirit of the early Christian communities must have been like: "All who believed were together and had all things in common; they would sell their property and possessions and divide them among all according to each one's need. Everyday they devoted themselves to meeting together in the temple area and to breaking bread in their homes. They ate their meals with exultation and sincerity of heart" (Acts 2:45). Like those early Christians, we worked, played, broke bread and embraced one another in the spirit of the commandment to "love your neighbour as yourself" (Mark 12:31).

## ENCULTURATING CATHOLIC CHARACTER

### Experience

Recount an occasion where you either experienced or witnessed the charitable love of one group of people toward another.

### Understanding

In what way is charitable love engendered by the virtue of solidarity?

### Reflection

(P) In what direction does your own sense of charitable love lead you?

(C) What is the charitable love that we, as a community, are known for?

### Reorientation

(P) Which group of people do you embrace in charitable love? How do you do that?

(C) How can we, as a school community, build an ethos of solidarity based on charitable love?

# VI. STEWARDSHIP

*Please follow the methodology outlined under the particular virtue of faith (or see the section entitled Methodology at the end of the book).*

I've always been puzzled by the juxtaposition of the concepts of "dominion" and "tilling" found in the two creation accounts in Genesis 1 and 2. Genesis 1 reads: "Then God said, 'Let us make humankind in our image, according to our likeness; and let them have dominion over the fish of the sea, and over the birds of the air, and over the cattle, and over all the wild animals of the earth, and over every creeping thing that creeps upon the earth'" (Genesis 1:28). Genesis 2 says: "The Lord God took the man and put him in the garden of Eden to till it and keep it" (Genesis 2:15). In our contemporary industrial-technological culture, having "dominion" connotes an air of dominance in the manner of some huge conglomerates that recklessly wreak havoc in the air, water and soil of our fragile ecosystem. They reap the benefits of the labour of others. This image stands in stark contrast to the humble gardener, who is in touch with the earth and knows the contours of the landscape. These passages present a troublesome dichotomy: we need to understand them in the contexts that they were written, in order to develop a notion of stewardship. We must strike a balance between "dominion," which in the biblical sense means an authentic source of authority, and the action of "tilling," which conveys an image of service. In our schools, we are certainly given dominion over our students, which indicates a certain level of authority and a concomitant level of responsibility, as expressed in our daily tilling of our students. It is in a synthesis of dominion and tilling that our students come to know they are worthy of cultivation.

# 49. SIMON THE GOOD STEWARD

Once while Jesus was standing beside the lake of Gennesaret, and the crowd was pressing in on him to hear the word of God, he saw two boats there at the shore of the lake; the fishermen had gone out of them and were washing their nets. He got into one of the boats, the one belonging to Simon, and asked him to put out a little way from the shore. Then he sat down and taught the crowds from the boat. When he had finished speaking, he said to Simon, "Put out into the deep water and let down your nets for a catch." Simon answered, "Master, we have worked all night long but have caught nothing. Yet if you say so, I will let down the nets." When they had done this, they caught so many fish that their nets were beginning to break. So they signaled their partners in the other boat to come and help them. And they came and filled both boats, so that they began to sink. But when Simon Peter saw it, he fell down at Jesus' knees, saying, "Go away from me, Lord, for I am a sinful man!" For he and all who were with him were amazed at the catch of fish that they had taken; and so also were James and John, sons of Zebedee, who were partners with Simon. Then Jesus said to Simon, "Do not be afraid; from now on you will be catching people." When they had brought their boats to shore, they left everything and followed him. (Luke 5:1-11)

Scripture informs us that Simon Peter was one of the first disciples Jesus chose. In Luke, Jesus asked Simon Peter to take him out from the shore so he could teach. Jesus then asked Peter to move to deeper water to cast his nets; respectfully, Peter said, "We have fished all night and caught nothing," but he did as Jesus asked, even when he wasn't sure of the reason. At our school we have our very own Simon, who has been fashioned in the image of St. Peter. His actions preach volumes in the shallow waters that our youngest children play in every day. Simon is their lifeguard: he watches over them, listens to them and ministers to them when they are in need. Each child begins his or her journey into the world by crossing the threshold of our school; there at the threshold, Simon is waiting to guide them into the inner sanctuary of our school and the deeper waters of human experience. We can only marvel at the mystery of our relationship with God and rejoice at its fruition in the interactions that occur each morning at the very human level of stuck zippers, lost socks and runny noses in the Junior Kindergarten room. Through it all we find the quiet but ever-present stewardship of Simon, which helps calm the waters. After his resurrection, Jesus commanded Peter to feed his sheep. Our Simon, literally and figuratively, feeds the sheep of our school each day. He dispenses milk to all the children at lunch, but more than that, these children find in him someone in whom they can confide. Just as St. Peter had difficulty at times, so, too, has our Simon. He is a tremendously gifted artist and is a strong visual and kinesthetic learner, but the demands of school do not always engage those gifts; undaunted by the challenge, he has found ways to use his gifts to overcome obstacles to learning that others don't have to face. Jesus said, "Blessed are the pure in heart" (Matthew 5:8); we say, "Blessed is the 'sacred heart' of our Simon."

## ENCULTURATING CATHOLIC CHARACTER

### Experience

Recount the story of a student who modelled the characteristics of the good steward to other students.

### Understanding

In what ways did the subject of your story exercise stewardship?

### Reflection

(P) In order to be a steward to others, you must be a steward to yourself. How do you exercise good stewardship toward yourself?

(C) What is our communal source of the deep waters of encounter with Christ?

## Reorientation

(P) One interpretation of the metaphor of the fishing net likens it to the early church that was gathering many new members. Which gifts of the Holy Spirit form the sinews of the net in which you gather others to the deeper waters of your encounter with Christ?

(C) How can we, as a school community, make sure that we feed the children in our care with the sustenance that comes from the deeper waters of our communal encounter with Christ?

# 50. "TJ," STEWARD OF
# THE IMAGINATION

**Then little children were being brought to him in order that he might lay his hands on them and pray. The disciples spoke sternly to those who brought them; but Jesus said, "Let the little children come to me, and do not stop them; for it is to such as these that the kingdom of heaven belongs." And he laid his hands on them and went on his way. (Matthew 19:13-15)**

I had an incredulous experience this week. A flight of Grade 1 children, in the manner of a small flock of fledgling birds suddenly descending from the skies to play a most marvellous melody, ever so softly graced the entrance to my office to proudly sing the notes of their great achievement. They had all taken home the infamous "TJ," an amiable bear who is known to inhabit the mid-highland region (second floor) of our school. Each had abducted him or her (it appears that the bear's gender is transmutable in different realms) for a short period of time to allow TJ to explore the inner regions of their homes and imaginations. It was delightful to hear the adventures of TJ in each of the stories that these young people proudly proclaimed from their journals. It captured the truly enchanting moments of both the classroom and the unfolding mystery of a child's mind, as it plays in the shadows between reality and pure fantasy. Each story introduced me to the culture, traditions and hopes of each of the children, as TJ traversed them all in his or her journey from their hearts to their heads. Thanks to all of you for providing opportunities for students to vicariously express who they are through the creative activities that you design, as embodied in the adventures of TJ.

## ENCULTURATING CATHOLIC CHARATER

### Experience

Share an activity that you use to engage the imaginations of the students in your care.

### Understanding

How can imagination be a way of coming to Jesus?

### Reflection

(P) What role does a sacred imagination (one that images God) play in your journey of becoming?

(C) What is the sacred image in our community's collective imagination?

### Reorientation

(P) What direction would your sacred imagination have you take in life?

(C) In what ways can our school community encourage a stewardship of sacred imagination in order to make known the way to the Kingdom?

# 51. SACRED FOOTPRINTS

When he established the heavens, I was there,
when he drew a circle on the face of the deep,
when he made firm the skies above,
when he established the fountains of the deep,
when he assigned to the sea its limit,
so that the waters might not transgress his command,
when he marked out the foundations of the earth,
then I was beside him, like a master worker;
and I was daily his delight,
rejoicing before him always,
rejoicing in his inhabited world
and delighting in the human race. (Proverbs 8:27-30)

I didn't quote the above proverb as a metaphor for the principal; I'm using it to praise our administrative professional, a.k.a. our beloved secretary. It is "wisdom" that resides with God, going forth as a "master worker." It should come as no surprise that wisdom is often personified in the feminine form. The feminine gods of many religious cultures are often personified in images connected to the earth. I know that our secretary has been my "master worker" from the first moment I assumed the role of principal. I have often tapped into her wisdom, and as a result, she has helped me avoid many of the potholes on the road that I must tread. I've also seen wisdom's other manifestations in her relationships with students, staff and parents, as steward and mother. It is in the stewardship of her earthly domain where, if you look closely, you can see her footprints pressed ever so lightly into the journeys of our most vulnerable students. Indeed, these are sacred footprints.

## ENCULTURATING CATHOLIC CHARACTER

### Experience

Recount a story that reveals how your beloved administrative assistant (or secretary) acted as the "master worker" in the school.

### Understanding

What role does wisdom play in stewardship?

### Reflection

(P) Does a sense of wisdom animate your life with feelings of delight? What is your delight?

(C) Where would we look to find sacred footprints in our community?

### Reorientation

(P) What role does wisdom play in the stewardship of students in your care?

(C) What measures can we take to ensure that we are building a communal sense of stewardship ("tilling" and "keeping" the soil of our "dominion") that is illuminated with the light of wisdom?

# 52. THE PONTIFICATOR

When he looked up and saw a large crowd coming toward him, Jesus said to Philip, "Where are we to buy bread for these people to eat?" He said this to test him, for he himself knew what he was going to do. Philip answered him, "Six months' wages would not buy enough bread for each of them to get a little." One of his disciples, Andrew, Simon Peter's brother, said to him, "There is a boy here who has five barley loaves and two fish. But what are they among so many people?" Jesus said, "Make the people sit down." Now there was a great deal of grass in the place; so they sat down, about five thousand in all. Then Jesus took the loaves, and when he had given thanks, he distributed them to those who were seated; so also the fish, as much as they wanted. When they were satisfied, he told his disciples, "Gather up the fragments left over, so that nothing may be lost." So they gathered them up, and from the fragments of the five barley loaves, left by those who had eaten, they filled twelve baskets. When the people saw the sign that he had done, they began to say, "This is indeed the prophet who is to come into the world." (John 6:5-14)

It was lunch hour and I was commemorating some of our past experiences with a supply teacher (a former student) as we watched the Grade 5/6s play intramurals. Suddenly, I was desperately summoned by one of our Grade 4 students to come immediately to her class. As I hurried toward the class, I thought I was about to enter a melee; I didn't know that I was about to enter the realm of the Holy Roman Empire, and that there I would find our Grade 4 teacher pontificating. Now, this is the last person I would have ever thought I would find pontificating in her classroom! After all, the term "pontificate" can refer to the office of the pontiff (noun) or to preside as a bishop (verb). But there is another meaning to discover. The root word comes from the stem of the mediaeval Latin word *pontificare*, which means bridge-builder. When I walked into the classroom, I observed two dozen architects about to burst in sheer delight, as their creations (bridges) groaned under the combined weight of their textbooks and creativity. It is only fitting that these architectural wonders were formed of spaghetti, penne and lasagna noodles. That makes sense gastronomically and etymologically, as the root of both pasta and pontiff brings us back to the heart of the Roman Empire and the pontifical seat of Rome itself. Thank God for the Italians! In the heart of this classroom was our own pontificator, the high priestess of intrigue and suspense – or should I say suspension (as in bridge). In the ecclesial sense of the word, our pope is the pontiff or bridge between God and the people of God. In our cultural context, our teacher was the high priestess bridging "becoming" and "being." In this sense, bridging is a special type of stewardship. It was as if the students had transformed seven bundles of "becoming" (the pasta of their creative potential) into twelve bridges of "being." This is the pattern of our spiritual journey, in which our process of becoming realizes being in the universe.

## ENCULTURATING CATHOLIC CHARACTER

### Experience

Recount a time when you witnessed students bursting with excitement about something they had created.

### Understanding

In what way was the engagement of their creativity giving them stewardship over their own becoming?

### Reflection

(P) What do you do to ensure that your life is one of becoming?

(C) What are we, as a community, becoming?

### Reorientation

(P) What bridge is creativity building in your life?

(C) How can we build a praxis (faith in action) of stewardship for a culture of becoming?

# HOW TO USE THIS BOOK

- Note that for the sake of clarity in the suggested methodology for each virtue, I use the term "General Virtue" to apply to the major classes of virtues (e.g., Theological, Cardinal and Communal) and the term "Particular Virtue" to refer to the different virtues within a general virtue (e.g., Faith, Hope and Charity).

- If you are using the book for personal reflection, I encourage you to record your questions, thoughts and feelings in a journal or on your computer or tablet as you go along. These thoughts can be the basis for further development and personal growth, should you choose to pursue a question, thought or feeling that is awakened in a reflection. I have included guidelines for journalling when we explore the theological virtue of faith (see Section I) as an example.

- If you are using the book with a group, have a facilitator lead the group through the reflections. The facilitator will read the description of the general and the particular virtue, as well as the text of the entire reflection, so he or she can make the connections between scripture, the narrative and the questions. The facilitator's role is key to providing the most enriching experience possible. I have also included guidelines for this activity when we explore the theological virtue of faith (see Section I) as an example.

## ELEVEN STEPS TO THE ENCULTURATION OF CATHOLIC CHARACTER

1. Begin the year by deciding on your plan for exploring these virtues. Here are two suggestions:

- Select one particular virtue to focus on for the entire year and simply use the four reflections for that virtue at four strategic times throughout the year; or

- Select one particular virtue per month. The monthly staff meeting would be a logical place to begin the reflection and the conversation about the focus for the upcoming month.

Note: The chaplaincy team, Catholicity team or faith ambassadors could be responsible for collating the suggestions that emerge from the staff meeting and coming up with a plan of action for the following month (or for the year, if only one particular virtue is selected). The team should invite other members of the community to participate in carrying out the plan.

Note: If you are doing this on your own, you can pick one particular virtue per month and read one reflection per week. There is no need to make a commitment to each of the particular virtues; rather, select only one or two to make a commitment to during the year. Quality is more desirable than quantity. In addition, your journalling could become part of your prayer life. For example, during the month dedicated to faith, you could begin with the prayer for an "act of faith," which will place you more completely in the presence of God; then you could meditate on and/or contemplate the gift of faith using the contents of your journals, in order to deepen your appreciation of God's grace in your life.

2.  Begin each reflection by reading the definition (to yourself or as a group) of the general virtue under which the particular virtue falls, to provide an overall context for the particular virtue.

3.  Define the particular virtue that is the focus of the reflection you are reading (located at the start of each group of four reflections) before reading its description.

4.  Read the description of the particular virtue for the reflection you are using.

5.  If needed, modify your definition of the particular virtue in light of the description you've just read.

6. Read the scripture quote, then pause to reflect on it. Try to identify a way in which the scriptural passage has a relevant message for you in your current circumstances, as related to the particular virtue you are exploring.

   - If you are in a group, allow time for group reflection and voluntary feedback.

   - If you are working on your own, journal your thoughts for ongoing reflection.

7. If needed, modify your definition of the particular virtue on the basis of the scripture passage.

8. Read the story and spend a few minutes reflecting on its message. Does the story strike a chord with your experience? If so, try to identify not only the chord, but also the underlying value. If not, does it strike a note of discord? If so, why?

   - If you are in a group situation, allow time for group feedback on a voluntary basis.

   - If you are doing this on your own, journal your thoughts for later reflection.

9. After the discussion or journalling is complete, take time to answer questions 1 (experience) and 2 (understanding). Record your responses; sometimes you will need to accommodate the method to differences in types of reflections.

   - If you are in a group, share your story with the group. If the group is large, divide into smaller groups and provide time for one story to be shared by each group. The facilitator should take time to connect the stories to scripture, the particular virtue and lived experience.

   - If you are doing this on your own, journal your thoughts for later reflection.

10. Now take time to record your personal (P) response to question 3 (reflection). This may not be an easy task, as it will require exploring unconscious thoughts, feelings or values.

- If you are in a group, time for sharing is provided, but not mandatory. (Note: Sharing is critical to forming community. Sharing is a form of intimacy where people make conscious for themselves and for others what they may have been unconscious of before. This sharing must be done with the same expectation of intimacy as when one shares with a friend; that is, with complete respect and confidentiality.) Some facilitators may choose to skip the personal discussion of question 3 and move to the community (C) question, but the thought process required for question 3 serves as a basis for question 4.

- If you are doing this on your own, journal your thoughts for later reflection.

11. Question 4 (reorientation) provides an opportunity to create a personal and/or communal consciousness of the orientation that you and/or the school might take in becoming more virtuous. Start by recognizing the ways in which you and/or the school have already established a culture of virtue. Then read the signs of the times, as it may be time to respond to new questions arising in yourself and/or the community or to adjust to cultural shifts that have occurred.

    - If the group is large, divide into smaller groups. These groups could script out their responses on chart paper and present them to the large group. After the presentations, the facilitator could identify a common or mutually agreed upon direction for the school community.

    - If you are doing this on your own, journal your thoughts for later reflection.

## METHODOLOGY

Each of the three main sections ("General Virtues") – the Theological Virtues, the Cardinal Virtues, and the Communal Virtues – is divided into a number of "Particular Virtues," For example, The Theological Virtues has three particular virtues: Faith, Hope and Love. Each particular virtue contains four reflections. Accompanying each reflection is an opening scripture quote; at the end of the reflection you will find questions and statements to explore. These questions and statements appear under the heading "Enculturating Catholic Character" and are divided into four processes: Experience, Understanding, Reflection, and Reorientation.

Below is a sample outline to follow as you work your way through the virtues we explore in the book. To make the book less bulky, I haven't repeated the methodology every time (although you will find it in the four reflections that form the first particular virtue in Section I, and in the first reflection in Sections II and III, to get you started). All you need to do is flip to this part of the book to refresh your memory as you delve into a new story.

# I. PARTICULAR VIRTUE (E.G., FAITH)

*Begin by reading the description of the general virtue under which the particular virtue falls (e.g., theological, cardinal or communal). Then write your own definition of the particular virtue in question.*

*Now read the description in the book (to yourself or as a group) before exploring any of the reflections under this particular virtue.*

*Then reconsider your definition of "faith": Is there anything you would change? If you are facilitating a group situation, allow time for participants to share their definitions in small groups. Ask the groups to come up with a definition of faith and then share it with the large group. Invite the groups to record their definitions for posting in a "Virtues" corner.*

## 1. REFLECTION (E.G., THE CHRISTMAS MIRACLE)

*Read the scripture quote.*

*Reconsider your most recent definition of the particular virtue. Is there anything you would change? Groups: Allow time for discussion and feedback to the large group. Individuals: Journal your response.*

*Read the story.*

151

*Reflect on the story*: Does the story strike a chord with your experience? If so, try to identify not only the chord, but also the underlying value. If not, does it strike a note of discord? If so, why?

- *If you are in a group situation, allow time for group feedback on a voluntary basis.*

- *If you are doing this on your own, journal your thoughts for later reflection.*

## ENCULTURATING CATHOLIC CHARACTER

### Experience

*Write your response to the statement under "Experience." If in a group, share your response with the group. Each group will select one story to share with the large group.*

### Understanding

*Talk to a friend or, if in a group, partner with someone who knows you, to answer the question. If in a group, on a voluntary basis, share your response with the group. Have each group, on a voluntary basis, share one response with the large group.*

### Reflection

*Write your response to the personal (P) question given under "Reflection." If in a group, on a voluntary basis, share your response with the group. Groups may, on a voluntary basis, share a story with the large group. The facilitator may skip the personal question and move to the community (C) question. Each group should be given the opportunity to share their response to the community question.*

### Reorientation

*Answer the personal (P) questions and, if in a group situation, the community (C) question. The facilitator will have each group report back to the main group. The facilitator may record the responses to the community (C) question and work toward a communal discernment of a praxis to which all are willing to make a commitment.*

# Essential Books for Catholic Educators

## Faith and Science Matters
*Edited by Fr. Rob Allore, SJ*
*Series edited by Michael O'Hearn*

Confronting misconceptions surrounding Catholic thought on various scientific developments, this collection of essays by leading scholars and educators helps us to understand Catholic teaching. Clear explanations offer us insights and ways to share the wealth of Church teaching on cosmology, creation, evolution, bioethics, ecology and technology.

**144pp PB 978-2-89646-407-4 $18.95**

The **Faith & Society Series** answers the burning questions of our time and shows Christianity's relevance to the many challenges of today's culture.

## It Began with a Promise: Demystifying Biblical Narratives for Teachers
*By Richard Olson*

With easy-to-understand explanations, narrative outlines and user-friendly guidelines, readers will gain greater insight into and a fuller appreciation of the Bible. Teachers, religious educators, and even parents will use this book as a resource for their own reflections and as a helpful reference for sharing the Scriptures with youth for years to come.

**128pp PB 978-2-89646-532-3 $14.95**

NOVALIS
www.novalis.ca

# Essential Books for Catholic Educators

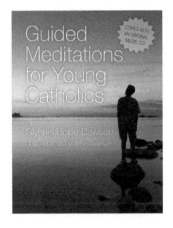

## Guided Meditations for Young Catholics
*By Glynnis Hope Dawson*
*Music by John Dawson*

Introduce intermediate-aged youth to the richness of prayer and meditation, and help them discover the many varied ways of praying. Perfect for catechists and religious educators, this exceptional collection of prayers and meditations not only teaches youth how to pray, but also invites them to consider important themes of Christian faith, such as the gifts and fruits of the Holy Spirit, the liturgical seasons, social justice and forming authentic relationships with others.

Complementing this compilation of prayers is a CD of music by John Dawson, one of Canada's foremost liturgical composers. Youth will be drawn more deeply into the meditations and discover the grace that daily reflection offers us.

**128pp PB with CD 978-2-89646-409-8 $29.95**

## Gifted by God: A Confirmation Retreat Kit
*By David Dayler & Anne Jamieson*
*Music by John Dawson*

Religious educators will welcome this wonderful kit for creating meaningful retreats for youth preparing for Confirmation. This retreat kit is an ideal companion to any sacramental preparation program, whether in the parish or school. It offers religious educators all the material — on a single DVD — needed for leading a retreat, including suggested schedules for full- and half-day retreats, leader's guide, prayer services, detailed activity plans, handouts and music.

**DVD and 4-Page Bklt 978-2-89646-546-0 $39.95**

# Catholic Education: Ensuring a Future
*By James T. Mulligan, CSC*

In *Catholic Education: Ensuring a Future*, Mulligan argues that everyone involved in Catholic education — parents and teachers, principals and superintendents, directors and trustees, priests and bishops — must own ever-greater responsibility and collaboration so that Catholic schools remain vibrant faith communities, offering students an authentic alternative to secular education.

**336pp PB 978-2-89507-671-1 $24.95**

# High School Ministry from A to Z
*By Brad Lewis*

Written for new campus ministers as well as seasoned ones, *High School Ministry from A to Z* is filled with energy, ideas, inspiration and passion. School administration, clergy and high school staff — who are all integral parts of high school ministry — will discover how this important ministry can connect to their classroom, office and role within the school.

**275pp PB 978-2-89646-036-6 $39.95**

NOVALIS
**www.novalis.ca**

# Essential Books for Catholic Educators

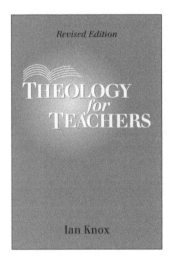

## Theology for Teachers
*By Ian Knox*

This book is for anyone interested in a comprehensive and accessible introduction to the Catholic faith. It is ideal for those who are preparing to teach in Catholic schools, as it fills the need for a basic text suited to the curriculum guidelines of the Institute for Catholic Education for university courses in Catholic education.

**384pp PB 978-2-89507-020-7 $29.95**

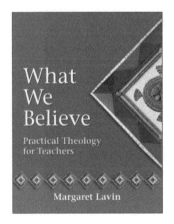

## What We Believe:
## Practical Theology for Teachers
*By Margaret Lavin*

If teachers are going to teach their faith, they need to know what it is about. *What We Believe* outlines the major theological themes that ground our understanding of who we believe God is, and who we are in relationship to God. *What We Believe* is the essential theological guide for all religious educators.

**174pp PB 978-2-89646-143-1 $24.95**

**Study Guide:**
**112pp PB 978-2-89646-144-8 $12.95**

**NOVALIS**
**www.novalis.ca**

# NOTES

# NOTES

# NOTES

# NOTES